Spilling the Beans

Martin Stott was born in 1954. He read geography at Mansfield College, Oxford, and gained his MSc from the London School of Economics. From 1977 until 1982 he worked as a founder member of the Political Ecology Research Group in Oxford. Since then he has worked for some years as a freelance writer and promoter of workers' co-ops and other local economic initiatives. He has published numerous articles in newspapers and journals including the *Guardian*, *Marxism Today*, *New Internationalist*, *Greenline*, *Resurgence*, *Vole* and *Political Quarterly*. He was a Churchill Fellow in the USA in 1984, and was recently appointed development worker with Oxfordshire Co-operative Development Agency. He is also a Labour councillor, representing Oxford's 'muesli belt' on the city council.

Martin Stott

Spilling the Beans

A style guide to the New Age

Fontana/Collins

First published in 1986 by Fontana Paperbacks
8 Grafton Street, London W1X 3LA

Cartoons by Bryan Reading
Photographs by Martin Stott

Set in Linotron Plantin

Made and printed in Great Britain by
William Collins Sons & Co. Ltd, Glasgow

Contents

Acknowledgements

A BOOK of this kind can only be written with a lot of help from friends. A number of my friends have given me continuous encouragement, support and good ideas. I'd particularly like to thank John Blackwood, Camilla Gugenheim, Trish Marsh, Andrew Morris and Rob Valentine, all of whom have assisted in ways which have ensured that this book actually happened. In addition I'd like to thank friends all over the country who read parts of it, added suggestions and sent clippings and stories to me while I was writing it, including Tony and Claire Golding, Liz Hosken, Chris Walker, Michael Richards, Laurence Golding, Maggie Eisner, Trisha Greenhalgh, Tom Sherry, Suzette Starmer, Jon Carpenter, Sarah Tyzack, April Marjoram, Eric and Jo Hodges, Paul and Marianne Birkitt, and my agent Maggie Hanbury, and many others who have requested anonymity. Valuable assistance was rendered to me while I was in California by Joyce Boyd and Roger Pritchard. Finally I'd like to thank Wendy Rimmer of Arrow Word Processing for helping get the text into a neat enough form to submit to the publishers.

Martin Stott
Oxford

Introduction

A new phenomenon has appeared. Suddenly at dinner parties or garden parties the most unlikely people start talking about their feelings, exchanging addresses of their acupuncturist or shiatzu teacher, announcing that they've become vegetarian or are giving up their jobs to run an organic smallholding, or declaring that they've joined the Green Party.

What is going on? Who are these people? How many of them are there? Estimates vary, but between 1½ and 3 million people are to a greater or lesser extent part of this trend – perhaps as much as 10 per cent of the adult population. Their average age is thirty-five. They are to be found all over the country but are more concentrated in the south and south-west than elsewhere. They are 'baby-boomers', children of the postwar era brought up on the welfare state, the 'you've-never-had-it-so-good' economic boom of the 1950s and, largely, the product of the 1960s expansion of higher education. They have benefited from all these trends, and have had the security to look at them critically. These are the Alternative Types (ATs) who may not be into self-sufficiency in Surbiton but have seen through all the materialist striving for bigger houses, faster cars, more expensive holidays, and better paid jobs – or they think they have. They are into self-exploration and voluntary simplicity. The 'outer directedness' of 'conspicuous consumption' has become the 'inner directedness' of the New Age.

Their basic attitudes stress self-development, non-aggression, emphasis of the feminine side of human nature to redress the existing imbalance. They lay store by the development of less ambitious, less planned, less competitive lifestyles. They exhibit an openness to the idea that there is an inner direction to events, that the right thing will happen if you allow it to. Influenced by a combination of 1960s radicalism, Eastern mysticism, and postindustrial greenish politics, their impact on Britain is just beginning to be felt. It is an amusing paradox that these 'anti-consumers' are now an identified and targeted trend among the advertising and marketing agencies, who correctly see them as sceptical consumers: innovative and influential, in some cases even trendsetters (e.g., in preventative health care), they are open to new products, but will not accept change for the sake of it, and will not succumb to the pressures of advertising.

All the traditional signs of success may have been rejected, but to *really* make it in the alternative world you need to know a much more subtle, until now unwritten, code. This book explains it all, how to score the maximum points for 'inconspicuous consumption', and without being *seen* trying to do so.

For those on the outside, this book explains who the ATs are, how they operate, what they feel and think, and how to spot one. Perhaps you're an aspiring AT or know someone who is. In the following pages, where all the examples really *are* true, you will be able to find out what to wear, where to live, what to 'do', what to call your children, the 'in' and 'out' therapies, holistic medical practices and gurus, and much more besides. This book will help you make the best possible impression when you join. It's a 'style guide' to the New Age, how to stay ahead, keep setting the trends, and impressing your friends. In short – how to win the first prize for non-competitiveness.

Where to live

London is a place to visit, not to live in. It's okay to go up for a weekend course, seminar sessions or those important events to be 'seen' at, and a plentiful supply of friends to stay with is therefore handy (they'll generally live in areas like Kentish Town, Tufnell Park or Dalston), but actually living there – no.

The area of Britain to live in is Devon. There are more natural healers, holistic health practitioners, alternative therapists and other inner-directed souls to the square mile in Devon than any other part of the country. South Devon is better than North Devon. The Totnes-Ashburton area is the veritable Californian Marin County of Britain. Living there is what all ATs ultimately aspire to. The south-west 'connection' as a whole has considerable chic extending to quite a wide area; other desirable places to live include:

Glastonbury (runs a close second to Totnes)
Stroud
Bath
around Cheltenham
and parts of Bristol

The next best area to live in is the Welsh/English border region, where house and land prices are still cheap enough for those aspiring to self-sufficiency. So common are ATs in this region that the Tory candidate in the 1985 Brecon and Radnor by-election was reported to be demanding 'urgent action' to deal with the 'hippie problem' in Powys during the campaign. He lost. Stretching up from the Forest of Dean, the most popular areas are:

Hay on Wye
Llandindrod Wells (ideal for collecting magic mushrooms in the autumn, this area has a *lot* of ex-hippies)
Kington

Presteigne
Welshpool
and west to
Llandidloes
Rhyader
Machynlleth (accessible for the Alternative Technology Centre)

Other concentrations are to be found in urban areas combining a certain amount of inner city decay and a multi-occupied housing stock, with a higher than average ex-student population. These areas have developed into their towns' 'muesli belts'. Places which have such quarters include:

Brighton
Oxford
Norwich and surrounding countryside

Leamington Spa (handy for acupuncture trainees)
Milton Keynes (New Bradwell only)
Telford (ATs savour living in Ironbridge, home of the Industrial Revolution and, they hope, the post-industrial one)

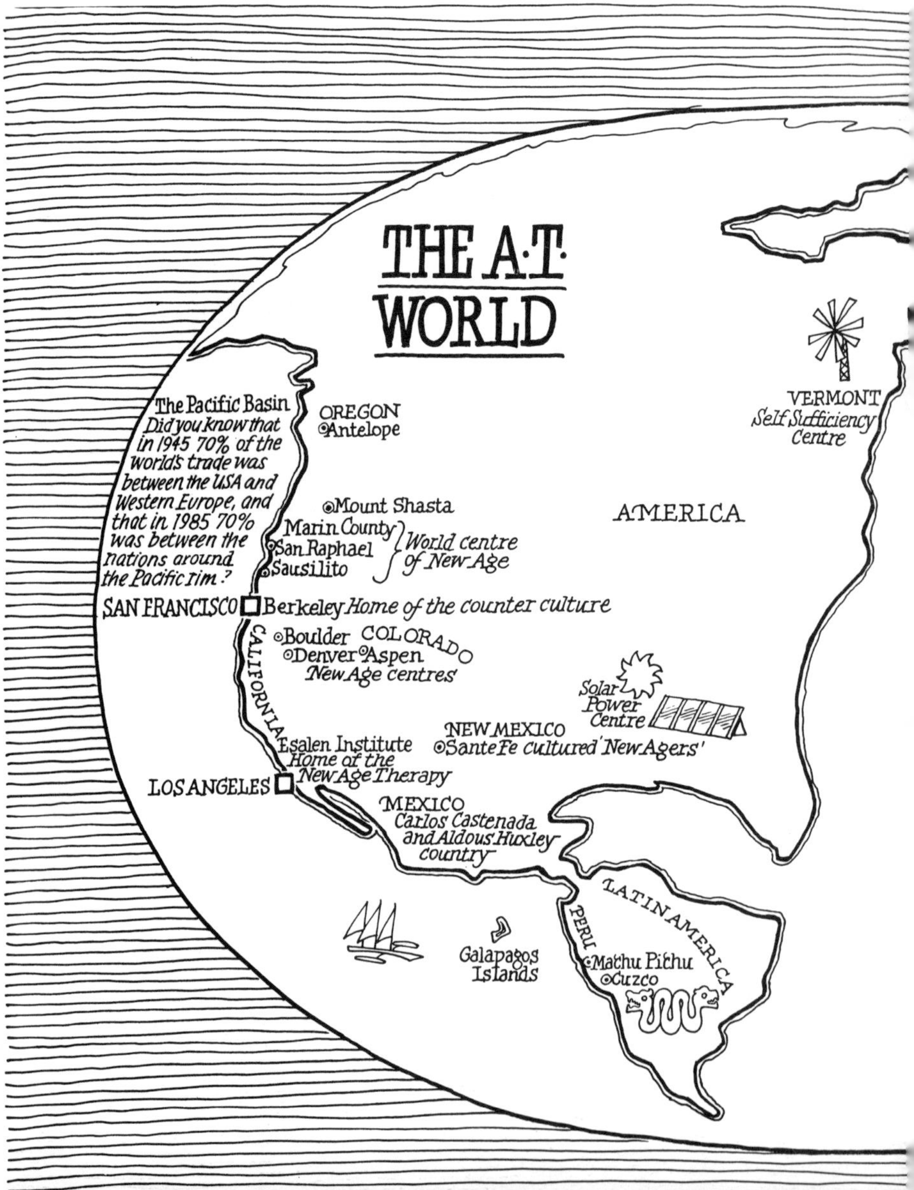

Hebden Bridge and other Pennine villages
parts of Leeds and Sheffield
Whitby
and Edinburgh

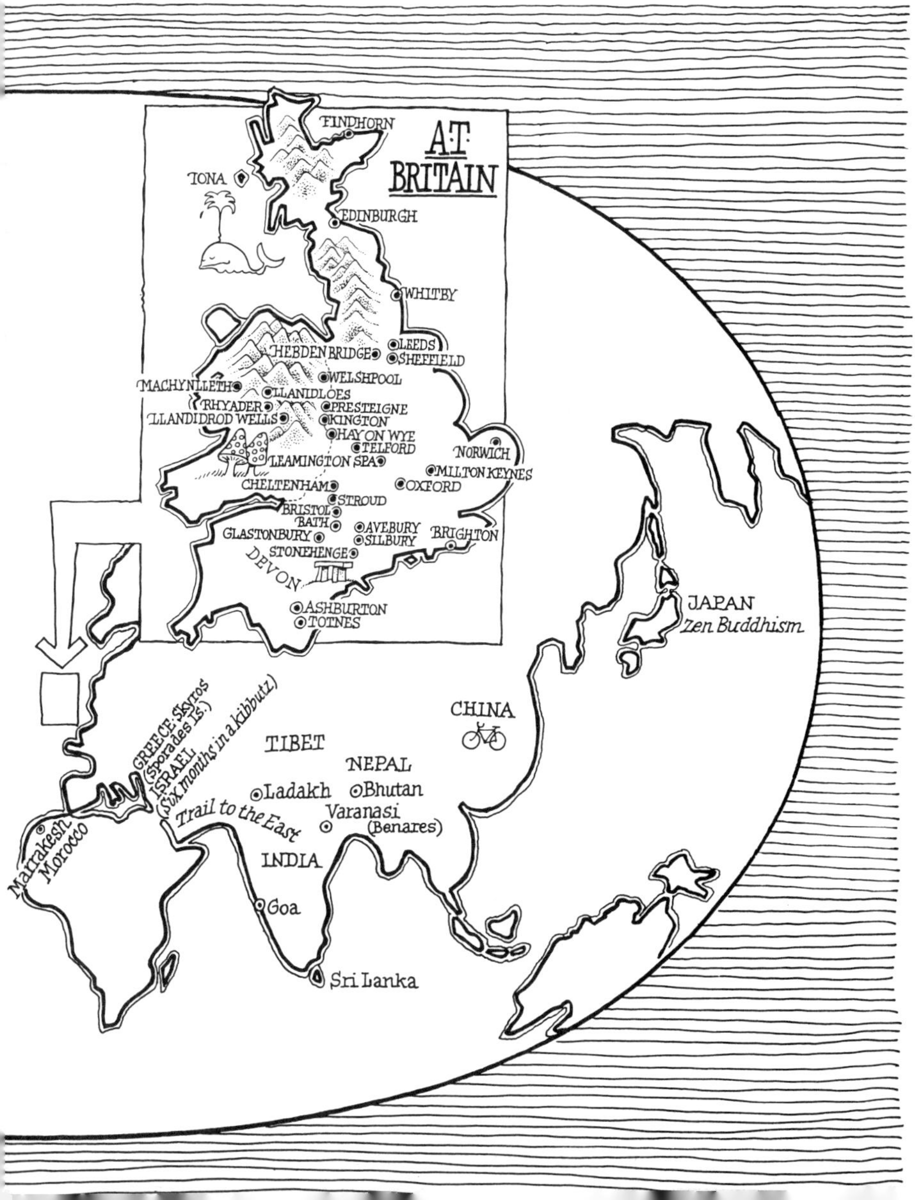

You know you are leaving AT territory when you spot your first jogger. 'Living in the country' is what all ATs aspire to (romantic visions of organic smallholding, hand-milking goats, woodburning stoves, alternative schooling for the children, hedgerows full of wild flowers, ethnic craftspeople nearby to supply needs you cannot provide yourselves, holistic health practitioner in nearest market town . . .) but if circumstances force them into an urban existence they will seek out, or if necessary create, their own 'muesli belt'. These areas are recognizable by the concentration of wholefood shops and cafés, alternative bookshops, cooperative printshops and national or local offices of campaigning charities, third world, ethnic and stripped-pine-furniture shops, a proliferation of bicycles and a multi-occupied housing stock with brightly coloured posters, stickers and curtains (and often bike shelters in the garden).

Street furniture will include spindly trees planted in unlikely places (a result of recently successful campaigns to 'green the city' by the well-supported Friends of the Earth group). There will be cycle lanes,

strange-looking bits of metal outside shopping parades (not modern art but a new design of cycle rack), various combinations of bollards, pavé-in-the-middle-of-the-road and metal barriers to close off residential streets to through traffic. Garish posters are flyposted on hoardings, calling for 'natural health on the national health' and suchlike things. Enormous, brightly painted vans and ambulances are parked in quiet sidestreets with peeling peace and anti-nuke stickers on them.

A quick peer at the 'personal ads' of the local post office will confirm all. You've clinched it if you see under 'accommodation wanted' a postcard saying something like:

> Aquarian ♂ psychology postgrad. seeks room shared in house/flat. Will live with carnivores, children, animals, smokers, or other tantric types . . . if they will live with me.

What do you 'do'?

In theory, ATs have abandoned the dualistic thinking behind such questions as 'What do you *do?*' After all, the way people earn their income these days may not be their guiding impulse in life, and in any case it implies a separation between economic and non-economic work, with excessive emphasis given to the economic. Nevertheless you'll get asked it so it's best to have an answer to hand.

For those who refuse to be categorized by their job, or who don't have the inclination to sell their labour, signing on is a very acceptable source of revenue, but only if you are doing something 'meaningful' with your life – training to be an acupuncturist, learning organic gardening or, if male, helping at the local crèche. AT men love to be *seen* looking after children.

For the rest, being 'in business' is not looked down upon at all (perhaps surprisingly). The traditional British attitude that there is something inferior about it has definitely been thrown out of the window. However you can't go into any old business. For the new breed of barefoot capitalist, 'right livelihood' and 'social responsibility' are the buzz words. Manufacturing riot control equipment can hardly be described as 'spiritually nourishing'. But this leaves plenty of scope for creating a need that nobody has ever thought of before, and 'doing well by doing good'.

ATs are known for thinking up several money-making schemes a week. So it's often not what you do but what you're about to start doing that counts, hence the importance of claiming (or its trendy mid-1980s alternative, the Enterprise Allowance Scheme). Many ATs are to be found in a variety of traditional jobs from postman to town-planner. If they are bored and alienated, they *dream* of their next move (and the money they will make as well as the satisfaction). If in one of the better paid professions, e.g. architecture, they fantasize about becoming the leading expert on passive solar heating systems, or similar – the AT expert on AT – but rarely get the chance.

The AT expert on AT

Here's a selection of possibilities to try when you get it together. Top of the list is anything to do with holistic health, natural healing or alternative therapy. Opportunities include:

Homeopath
Polarity therapist
Intuitive masseur
Iridologist
Reflexologist
Metamorphic therapist
Aromatherapist
Alexander technique teacher
Naturopath
Acupuncturist
Herbalist
Stress-reduction consultant

Any of the 'short order' psychotherapies do well too:

Transpersonal psychologist
Reichian therapist
Gestalt therapist
Bio-energetics teacher

Creating your own New Age derivatives of these leads to opportunities like:

Psychophilosopher ('activate your Karmic birthright through the realization of your life's work, explore issues such as values, talents, passions, skills, achievements, directions, and strategies')

Barefoot capitalism closely reflects the AT's musical tastes

Rebirther (great opportunities here – rebirthers claim to initiate miraculous changes in your life, at work, at home, in your relationships, your money matters, and in your view of yourself, all through breathing. As with all cure-alls, it comes expensive to the client)

Astrologer (personal, *not* for the newspapers)

Enrolling in the twelve-year 'Geshé programme' (at the Manjushri Institute, Cumbria, and drop out after one year)

Right Livelihood

Mulla Nasrudin used to stand in the street on market days, to be pointed out as an idiot. No matter how often people offered him a large and a small coin, he always chose the smaller piece.

One day a kindly man said to him, 'Mulla, you should take the bigger coin. Then you will have more money and people will no longer be able to make a laughing-stock of you.'

'That might be true,' said Nasrudin, 'but if I always take the larger, people will stop offering me money to prove that I am more idiotic than they are. Then I would have no money at all.'

Those with more self-confidence try setting up as 'Guru' (this began as an Eastern vocation, but recently it has become a popular Western profession). People who write cultish New Age books are soon adopted as gurus. Frequently American, e.g. Marilyn Ferguson (author of *The Aquarian Conspiracy*) or Fritjof Capra, these 'flying gurus' do world trips. When they visit, the thing is to be on the specially invited guest list. A lot of fun can be had getting into the 'inner circle'.

Manufacturing and supplying the equipment and other spin-off products for the new breed of healers opens up opportunities too. Try any of these:

herbal creams, cleansers, tonics and moisturizers (look at the size of The Body Shop, a real AT success story)
air ionizers for home and office
aerobics bouncers
water distillers
fruit juicers and associated
beechwood pressing blocks
aura goggle manufacturers (for seeing people's psychic energy)

For the traditional craftsmen and skilled worker new opportunities are opening up fast: wind chime and Gamelan chimes production for the musical instrument maker, alternative energy installations (solar panels, windmills, methane gas digestors, linked to compost toilets) for plumbers and electricians (now renamed 'intermediate technologists'). Carpenters can turn their hands to birthing chairs, massage tables and meditation stools.

Organic garden products are also a growth sector. Selling wild flower seeds looks like a good bet for the future. For those who *really* take the organic bit seriously and can cope with dispensing with creature comforts, becoming a self-sufficient peasant is very acceptable. It usually doesn't last more than about four years, though. The move back from the Welsh hills to Islington has begun.

The Holistic Multinational

Mystical tour operators, wholefood shops and cafes, occult, esoteric and spiritual bookstores . . . the empire can soon grow. The small town of Glastonbury has spawned a veritable 'alternative multinational' – The Glastonbury Experience Ltd. 'Divisions', as they're known, of this experiential conglomerate include a natural health clinic, a tour operator, alternative bookshop, cafe and wholefood shop.

Of the traditional professions, being an enlightened GP is probably the best, especially if feminist in perspective. They practise homeopathy on the NHS (so as not to be upstaged by the 'natural' healers) and provide their patients with interminable prophylactic questionnaires with mystical questions like 'Who is responsible for your health?'

Professional services

A whole host of professional services are in existence or can readily be developed to service these new entrepreneurs and their clients. Perhaps one of these would suit:

- financial adviser on socially responsible investing
- counselling on the relief of guilt generated by the inheritance of wealth
- space harmonizer ('Do you feel nurtured by your personal space? Does your environment allow you really to be yourself? The spaces we create are tailored to your activity pattern, personality, expression and requirements for inner peace')

Naming your business

Barefoot capitalists – a new breed – are much more creative in their business names than their barefaced contemporaries like Exxon and ITT. Try these for size:

Pie in the Sky
Home on the Range
Alice's Restaurant
} (wholefood restaurants)

Cycloanalysts
Lunar Cycles
} (bike repair)

In Stitches (clothing manufacturers)

Brixton Mortar
Being and Nothingness
} (building co-ops)

Wet Dreams (everything for your bath . . . and after)

Gentle Ghost (removals)

Aquarian Agency (New Age management consultants)

Maggie's Farm
Dharma Distribution
} (wholefood and organic wholesalers)

Karma Kanic ('We're here to help you deal with what seems to be the foundation of life today, your car, in an enlightened and wholistic manner')

- running seminars on 'winning at work' (integrate the principles of personal growth with your current ways of getting results at work)
- running courses on barter as a form of trade ('discover your own money attitudes, your own barterable skills, learn key bartering techniques')
- 'new games' trainer (cooperative and non-competitive games)
- networker (especially if 'networking the networks')
- 'inner game' tutor
- vision consultant (not a fancy name for your TV repairman, or even your optician, but someone who clarifies your 'vision' of yourself and your future)

The business card

It is still considered a bit pretentious by most people to have a business card in Britain unless you are a scrap-metal dealer or a senior executive in a multinational corporation. But being on the 'leading edge' of change, ATs have taken them to their hearts. Cards are an essential element of any 'right livelihood' business in the United States, and are rapidly becoming so here. Here are the key elements that make up a successful card:

- Keep it small (outsize cards are difficult to carry about)
- Display your trading name, address and phone number clearly
- Keep the description of your product or service to no more than six words
- Incorporate in the design of your business logo a meaningful New Age symbol, such as:
  Yin/Yang symbol
  Something from the I Ching
  Eternal flame
  Tree of life
  Celtic knots
  Some modification of the caduceus
  (particularly suitable for natural healers)
  Something on the theme of the heart
  Sun, moon, stars

An astrological symbol
Symbolic representation of a sea shell, opening flower, bamboo shoot etc.
As a last resort, something in Chinese or Japanese calligraphy (like a cleverly designed £ sign)

Networking: the new fad

Back in prehistory, before the New Age put us all right on this, people used to meet together at parties, seminars, conventions, rallies and other occasions, and in between the formal bits, over lunch or coffee in the bar, at the back of the hall, or in the corridors they used to talk to people, exchange ideas, names, addresses, mutual contacts or the titles of the latest books or articles. No longer. All this happy and productive activity has been replaced by a new science – NETWORKING.

Every time you pick up the telephone and dial a number, write a letter, check your address book, subscribe to a magazine or journal, press a button on your computer, tune up on your CB radio, receive a visitor in your office, or go and visit someone yourself, you are participating in this new science – you're NETWORKING.

Ever since the first cave people scratched pictures of mammoths and antelopes on the cave walls people have been communicating information about themselves and their world to other people, but only recently have all these activities been recognized for what they truly are – NETWORKING.

Networking fulfils all the criteria that are needed to make it an ideal activity for the AT – it's decentralized, it's non-hierarchal, it's 'people-centred', it's convivial technology, and most important a simple everyday activity, is magically transformed by a little redefinition into the latest New Age cult. Futures 'experts' inform us that it's one of the 'megatrends' shaping our lives. Books have been written about it, networking magazines abound, there even exists a Networking Institute to study the new phenomenon and develop theories about it. It's a determining characteristic of the 'leading edge', a future which is all about 'the shift from mass to information'.

It can have a much simpler meaning. Networking can be less of a grand theory and more of a way of ensuring an endless supply of free lunches. Imagine the scene. It's a dark, windswept and rainy October evening. You're sitting happily in front of your TV watching *Dr Who* and sipping a cup of Barleycup . . . There's a knock at the door. You stumble out of the room, unbolt the catches, turn on the outside light, and there, standing on the doorstep, are two dripping strangers with enormous backpacks.

Says one (male), 'Is this where Jim Costello lives?'

'Yes,' you say uncertainly, 'that's me.'

'Oh, great,' says the stranger, in an accent you now recognize as Australian. 'We met a friend of your sister's boyfriend Max at Glastonbury back in June. He said we could drop by any time if we were in the area and stuck for a place to crash.'

They begin to shift their packs towards you. A momentary expression of panic crosses your face. You look at the driving rain, and stutter, 'Oh yes . . . nice to see you . . . do come in . . . '

Five minutes later, pools of water on the kitchen floor, packs steaming gently in the corner, they are sprawled in your living room tucking into the last of your bread and cheese, and eyeing your stereo and record collection. They give every impression of settling in for a long stay. They do.

They are networking.
You are the networkee.

The New Age

MATT BLACK

It is the age of being,
considerate.
When my friends call for tea
on Sunday afternoon
after walking in the rain
they bring mud
on their feet
and put it
on the carpet.

So it doesn't have to wait
outside,
getting wet.

'Saving the world'

Politics is not a word that's heard too much around the AT set. People with 'grand designs' are looked at with some scepticism, and ATs' political views range right across the spectrum from right-on to right-wing. As a consequence, joining parties isn't really done, but getting heavily involved in causes is.

These are the current favourites:

- Anything 'green'
- Greenpeace (though you're concerned about the effects of their seal and whale campaigns on the Eskimo's and Canadian Indian's indigenous culture)
- Green Deserts (involved in planting trees in the Sahara to reverse desertification)
- Green CND
- Friends of the Earth
- Animal rights groups
- And the only party political exception: the Green Party

Worrying about the diminishing ozone layer, acid rain in Scandinavia, the destruction of the Amazon rain forest, the destruction of Aboriginal lands in Australia, Latin America or Southern Africa or anything else that you can't do anything about is quite okay.

Other areas to get involved in include campaigning about:

additives in food
multinational drug companies' policies in the third world
human rights (Amnesty International is a good thing)
natural childbirth
alternative education (You can be a pillar of your Education Otherwise group. This is the 'having your cake and eating it' approach to education. You can avoid sending your children into the grubby council school *and* sneer at the class-divisiveness of those who put their little darlings in the private sector.)

Feminism (especially if male)
Proportional representation (even though you don't understand the effects of the different systems)
Nationalism (if Scottish or Welsh resident)

A regular banker's order to War on Want is quite trendy these days, and salves the conscience; or alternatively a subscription to *New Internationalist*. An armchair approach to anarchism is a good position to take up. It enables you to criticize both socialists and capitalists without ever having to risk your own extremely vague ideas being put to the test. A robustly critical attitude towards multinational corporations, especially pesticide and drug manufacturers, the food industry and those involved in the nuclear fuel cycle (which just about covers the lot), should be combined with an equally hostile attitude towards traditional socialist ideology. Attack this from the 'small-is-beautiful – decentralization' or 'nationalization-doesn't-make-the-industries-more-responsive-to-workers/consumers-needs' directions. The nearest you ever got to a 'big picture' approach was as a student when you joined SCM (Student Christian Movement – much more radical than its name suggests). For those with more of a social conscience, calling yourself a socialist in the right circles is still okay,

Sharing the global perspective

though you run the risk of being accused of advocating 'hobbit socialism' by your left critics.

Attitudes on these matters are not uniform. There's a 'spiritual tendency' among ATs who see 'the multinational corporation as an agent of positive transformation'. Holding to the view that people's misfortune is their own fault, that if they gave out the right energy they would receive back all they needed, and that the 'wealth-creating' activities of multinationals has 'led to the greater diversity of the human potential movement' is quite acceptable among this group. Some also claim to be 'transpolitical', i.e., beyond the divides that separate merely ordinarily politically inclined folk.

Back in 1968, 'revolution' might have been on everyone's lips, but these days it sounds terribly dated, and you run the risk of being mistaken for a 'headbanger'* if you use it. Remember, '*revolution*' is out, '*transformation*' is in.

* Trans: 'headbanger' – derisive term used to describe Militant Tendency supporters particularly by other members of the Labour Party.

The New Politics

Back in the summer of 1981, the City University in London hosted the 'First Assembly of the Fourth World', a real AT gathering if ever there was one. The *fourth* world, for those only familiar with three, is 'small nations, communities and the human spirit'. The proceedings of the assembly were published in a book unblushingly entitled *How to Save the World*. This extract from one of the floor contributions gives some idea of the style of political language needed to complement 'the new politics'. It's about the practical problems of decentralization – an important subject for aspiring AT politicians.

> It's important for us to descend down into our centre somewhere here [raised palm slowly drops to solar plexus], and that this dimension of the fourth world has to do with the transformation of our modes of perceiving ourselves, a transformation of our consciousness, for an evolution of our consciousness. You could call it an expansion into fuller levels of awareness, of understanding of ourselves, of one another, socially, and of the earth, the Earth Mother, Gaia, of which we are a part, ecologically, if you want to use those terms. And with that the necessity to have, somehow, the tolerance and the receptivity for the emergence of new symbols that are struggling to be born. And indeed new rituals in order to focalize our new understanding of collective unity (from *Vole*, vol. IV, no. 8, September 1981).

Got it?

Role models

Everyone needs heroes, but the term is suspect, so we talk of 'role models'.

'Top of the Pops' is undoubtedly:

Fritz (E.F.) Schumacher ('Small is beautiful' is one phrase that really has entered into common currency).

Followed by:

Gandhi
Martin Luther King
Buckminster Fuller (radical futurist, inventor of geodesic domes)
Chief Seattle (nineteenth-century Indian Chief whose thoughts on humankind's relationship to the natural world are much quoted, including in the Ecology – now Green – Party's 1983 manifesto)
Krishnamurti (anti-guru, discovered by Theosophists in India in the early part of this century)
Pooh Bear (star of *The Tao of Pooh*)
John Lennon
Wilhelm Reich (much misunderstood psychoanalyst now gradually being rehabilitated)

Lesser gods and goddesses (all still alive) include:

Hazel Henderson (*the* alternative economist)
Prince Charles (vegetarian, organic farmer, and patron of holistic medicine)
Fritjof Capra (inventor of new physics)
Petra Kelly (leading member of German green party)
John Seymour (101 ways with self-sufficiency)
R. D. Laing (anti-psychiatrist)
Ivan Illich (social critic, author of books like 'tools for conviviality')
Theodore Roszak (the counterculture's official biographer)

Actually *knowing* a role model conveys a great deal of kudos. It enables the creation of a new genre – alternative name-dropping. A classic is 'Gandhi taught me to spin'; which indicates that it wasn't just a passing acquaintance, and the story can't be disproved as he's been dead almost forty years.

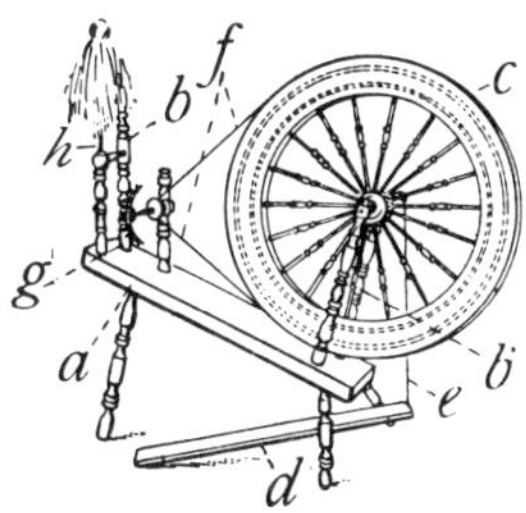

Essential vocabulary

Nothing identifies an AT more clearly than the way he or she speaks. A whole new lexicon has been developed by ATs to describe the world and their place in it. This 'new brutalism' that ATs have imposed on the language has largely been imported from the USA but has rapidly taken root here.

AT people are the 'leading edge' of the 'New Age' which they define as 'an evolutionary concept of Mankind (sic) being on the point of ascending to a higher state of being'. A handy substitute for 'New Age' is 'Aquarian Age' (we're in 'the dawn' of it), and the process by which we're moving into it is known as a 'paradigm shift'. ATs' thinking is defined by this 'new paradigm'. Dictionaries describe 'paradigm' as meaning 'example' or 'pattern'; for ATs, however, 'new paradigm' is just a phrase used to impress. When pressed to define it, New Age 'thinkers' simply make up their own definition on the spot: something like 'a new vision of reality' or 'world view'. But of course defining anything is 'dualistic' or 'left brain' (bad words: to describe anything or anyone as 'dualistic' or 'left brain' is, in short, damnation).

This 'world view' has spawned all sorts of new concepts. Front-runner among these is 'Gaia', a word that's being absorbed into the everyday language at remarkable speed. Use of it indicates a 'holistic' (in American sp. 'Wholistic') approach to life. 'Gaia' means seeing the planet as one interdependent living organism. 'Planet' or 'planetary' is a crucial new term. Political action is seen in planetary terms, as in 'planetary initiative for a world *we* choose' (what about the choices of the rest of us non-ATs?), which is a handy portmanteau to avoid taking *any* substantive political action. 'Think globally, act locally' is the slogan of this movement, and the term 'global village' is on everybody's lips. The end of all this activity is supposed to be global and personal transformation (very important to link the two).

For those who can't cope with trying to save the entire world

single-handedly, there are smaller geographical areas now available. These are known as 'bio-regions'. The Mediterranean is a bio-region, so is the Sahel, and use of the term indicates a rejection of shallow and divisive concepts such as nation or class, and a transcendent internationalism.

At work you're interested in 'empowerment'. If you're an employer you 'empower' your employees (though not by doing anything 'meaningful' like giving them trade union rights). This process will lead to greater 'abundance' (profits, success) for your firm, and 'nourishment' for yourself (an all-round feeling of well-being for doing the right thing).

Being interested in the 'spiritual harmony' of your employees, you want to make their 'participation' in your business 'meaningful' and 'rewarding'. This is done through the institution of 'quality circles' (opportunities for the management to steal good ideas from the workforce) and 'employee participation' (making sure the management stays firmly in charge). When the business goes under, it hasn't failed; you've had a 'learning experience'.

Therapy of various kinds has had a profound influence on AT

language. 'Therapy-speak' has an unfortunate tendency to use candour in order not to be candid.

Thus you 'make connections' with people rather than falling in love like everyone else. Once involved, you have a 'scene' or a 'relationship' (what *kind* of relationship is never made entirely clear) with the other person. Conversation in this context is out. 'Sharing' is in (particularly 'sharing your feelings'). In fact feelings are so vital that it's quite okay to put people down by insisting on the primacy of 'feelings not facts'. This is a great way of seeming open without being so. Using the phrase 'it feels' rather than 'I think' will gain you a lot of points (as in 'It feels as if you haven't done the washing-up for ages'). 'Getting in touch with . . . your feelings' is a crucial part of life. It's what you spend all that money on therapy for, so that at the end you'll be able to 'relate to' or 'connect with' your partner on a much more deeply 'spiritual level'. If things don't go well, you'll find you'll want more 'personal space' (time on your own) because of the 'bad vibes' you've been getting. However the success or failure of a particular 'relationship' is part of your 'Karma', so just 'go with the flow' and whatever's supposed to happen will.

Recent therapy graduates come out with stunning banalities which in the euphoria of the moment seem (to them) like profundities: 'Did you know that most of the time we barely breathe' (that could be a rebirther looking for another opportunity to be 'prospered'); or to their 'partner', 'I hear you' (which means, 'I'm not listening to what you're saying'), or 'What's going on for you?' (which means, 'I'm so emotionally mixed up after all this I can't tell what the hell I feel, but that's not what's supposed to happen, so I'll project it on to you').

New phrases creep into their language, for example 'quality time'. This is supposed to be those periods when they 'spiritually connect' (i.e. more intensely) with one another (as opposed to those times when they merely 'connected' or watched TV together); in reality it is no more than an elaborate excuse for spending less time with each other.

The recently therapized often show a touching faith in the abilities of the 'facilitator' of their workshop. The more spiritually inclined sessions will have 'focalizers' and are generally preceded by 'attunement sessions'.

The 'new brutalism' isn't confined merely to language; the natural healers' 'scene' has taken to assaulting the very spelling of words so now you can pay enormous sums to engage in:

- 'pharsting' (millions do it in Africa and India all the time but it's spelt differently over there)
- or 'bodi-klensing' (what people used to do in a tub in front of the coal fire on a Saturday night).

Making simple things complicated is a reliable touchstone; after all, language isn't supposed to facilitate communication, it's meant to terrorize or impress people. This is easy enough to do. Think of a simple everyday concept or object and redefine it. Thus the humble clothes-line is magically transformed into a 'solar drier'* with all the buzz-word connotations in the listener's mind – natural energy sources, appropriate technology, voluntary simplicity . . . try it yourself.

One of the problems with 'AT-speak' is that some words and phrases may be popular for a few years, but are so outrageous that even the most credulous stop using them and they go out of fashion. Here's a handy guide to some of those words and phrases you *shouldn't* be heard using:

- 'mellow out' (relax)
- 'flash' (as in 'flashing' on something – having a good idea)
- 'catch rays' (meaning unclear – *translator*)
- 'boogie' (something like 'let's party')
- 'bummer' (bad drug experience)
- 'lay raps' (as in laying raps on someone, or arguing with them)
- 'get wasted'
- 'get behind'
- 'where are you coming from?' (unless at bus or train station)
- 'head' (as in 'head shops')
- 'cosmic'
- 'far out'
- 'too much'
- 'no hassle'

* Advertisers, note: this concept not available in Wales, the west, the north, Scotland or Ireland.

Next time you're networking at a New Age event, listen out for the conversation, or see how many buzz words you can insert into your own opportunity to 'share'. Score one point for each word. Here are three examples of what can be done in quite limited space. Remember when you do it, it's not just the words you use but the context and the way you use them that will impress the judges.

> The idea is to give people an opportunity for meeting *like-minded souls* and to *share* the *leading edge* topics dealing with our *personal* and *global transformation* . . . every Monday night remains my *spiritual* and *emotional bath* because that's where I meet *my kind of people:* willing to *change* themselves before they advocate change in others. In an attempt to offer *food* for the *whole person, body, mind and soul*, we always introduce ourselves to our neighbours at the beginning of the meeting and go to the wine bar afterwards where we *strengthen our connections* with each other (*Resurgence*, no. 107, November 1984).

> The place for *transformation* is *incarnated* in Venice. The close *relationship* necessary for the *symbolic spiritual* fire of the winged lion and the *feminine* water, where the *creative seeds* germinate, will happen with imposing force. The whole, a *planetary centre* with the qualities specific to its very nature: 'to indicate the *path of beauty* in civilization'. Attention and creative *energy* are *convoked* for the creation of '*spheres of planetary vision*', with *systems and modalities* which differ remarkably from the *common logic of exchanges*, where human relationships are means of interest rather than the *understanding and fulfilment* of the *human role* in life. He who gives thanks, and he who receives, in the very same act, distributes a *greater energy* than that which has *nourished him*. In the *centres of global vision* the *whole and the part* make the *vibratory qualities* of the *organism* excel in every act (brochure on the Venice Planetarium of the Arts, 1985).

> Our aim is to provide a venue where we can meet, *interact, learn* from each other's *visions*, and discover the *vital relationships* that are shaping the economic landscape of the 80s and 90s. It is our hope that by the end of the conference everyone will have been *nourished* and *empowered* to live a more *meaningful* and *abundant* life (advertisement for the 'New Economic Agenda' Conference, Findhorn, October 1984).

Congratulations to all three contestants.

Relationships

Love

To most people, falling in love means falling in love with *someone else*. This isn't the case with ATs: they fall in love with themselves and have *relationships* with other people. All ATs know that you'll never have a successful 'relationship' unless you love yourself first; that's why they 'work on themselves' so much of the time, lavishing their care and attention on their spiritual, emotional and bodily well-being.

Nevertheless, the same careful approach has to be taken with 'relationships'. The hunt for the perfect soul mate is a major project, perhaps even a lifelong endeavour, not to be undertaken in a spirit of levity. How do you do it? These days there are all sorts of ways, tried and tested, to help you along the path. Why not try:

- 'Divine connections' ('Spiritual match-making and relationships service')
- 'Magical matching' ('Weary from connecting with impossible mates? Soul mates really exist who are ready to share your same emotional, spiritual and psychic qualities')
- 'Inner journey facilitation' ('This technique is not for everyone, but only those with courage and strong desire to do *whatever it takes* to have their soul mate')
- Astro-cartography (Not confined exclusively to affairs of the heart, the astro-cartography computer generates an individual map of the world from your birth data, identifying every locality where planets are influential. Hundreds have reported happily meeting love mates where *Venus* crosses their map)

There's a great tendency among ATs to greet people by hugging them, so much so that it's become a completely meaningless form of social contact. If you're *really* interested in someone, they'll be much more convinced if you throw convention to the wind and *shake their hand*.

Sex

Once you've hit on someone to have a 'meaningful relationship' with, the question of sex arises. These days, with AIDS, Herpes and other 'risk factors' so widespread, you cannot be too careful. The AT's approach to sex is remarkably conservative: nothing kinky, none of this goal-orientated search for the 'big O' or the 'G-spot', or trying out exotic positions or commercial gimmicks. Sex is a spiritual activity, the meeting on the physical plane of two cosmic entities. Sociologists more eminent than I refer to this tendency as the 'sacrilizing of sex', and it must be treated as such – seriously. 'Having sex' is out. You 'make love' *with* and not *to* somebody.

Some ATs go for tantric sexual practices – hours of penetration without orgasm. Very cool.

Monogamy is in (strictly, serial monogamy, i.e. people change partners every few years in line with their self-development).

Heterosexuality is in (though so is lip-service to bisexuality) and celibacy is in (some ATs influenced by Eastern thought reckon sex isn't necessary). Being gay is okay as long as you have a stable partner (the AIDS scare has narrowed options dramatically). Sleeping around, so-called 'free love', might have been okay for men in the 'liberated' days of the counterculture, but feminism has put an end to those double standards (mostly).

Feminism has also led to the development of the 'New Age man'. This much-hyped creature will be aged under thirty-five, gentle, caring, uncompetitive, almost androgynous, loyal and emotionally strong to his female companion; he'll be a dab hand at everything from sex to salads – perhaps even involving the two – and will belong to a 'men's group' so as not to become emotionally dependent on women. They often have beards (especially the older ones). Some feminists don't believe that this creature really exists, reckoning that he is worse than the traditional sexist man because he is more skilled at concealing his true nature.

Contraception is a tricky area. Men may have walked on the moon, but there is still no safe and easy form of contraception for women. Lip-service is paid to taking equal responsibility, but the sheath, although used, isn't that popular and there isn't anything else around for men. Vasectomy is too hi-tech. So once again it falls on women. The pill is out, IUD has a lot of question marks over it, leaving the cap, and other more hit-and-miss remedies like natural contraception and 'astro-contraception' (organizing your sexual practices around the phases of the moon). These systems ensure a baby every year – for a time.

LTRs

ATs don't get married, they have LTRs. This is not the latest form of video equipment from Japan, but a 'long-term relationship'. It will be entered into with some care, and will be signalled by some form of 'commitment ceremony'.

In reality marriage is still an acceptable form of 'commitment ceremony'. Quaker marriages are undergoing a revival, and it's okay too if you belong to an obscure religion like Greek Orthodoxy or Roman Catholicism – you can go in for the whole works, three-hour sung nuptial mass, candles, incense, banks of flowers, massed choir (and a cast of hundreds of awe-struck guests, most of whom won't have been in a church for years). For those who want to break out of this mould, alternative 'rites of passage' (the new generic phrase for these activities) are now becoming available. You can write your own ceremony, recite poems, invite cherished friends to give speeches, and have a fiesta. It's by no means unknown for startled friends and relatives to receive invitations from the couple's *child* inviting them to the wedding of his/her parents, these days. Choosing a venue is important:

- Mayday on the village green round a maypole has suitable 'fertility rite' connotations and goes down well.
- Ancient sites associated with the goddess of fertility have the right 'energy'. Try the Cerne Abbas giant in Dorset, or Silbury Hill in Wiltshire (the hill is supposed to be the pregnant belly of the earth goddess).

These days you can even get professional assistance. 'Rites of Passage Inc.' offers a week's 'vision quest' to help you create your own ceremony. Presents need not be too elaborate: wild flowers, bottles of homemade wine, a small handmade object are fine. For the more sophisticated the rule is 'software not silverware'.

All this lavishing material goods on the happy couple is *out*. Producing a formal present list is extremely uncouth, and dividing it up among posh London shops is a pastime only indulged in by Sloanes (or aspiring Sloanes).

One problem with LTRs is that quite a few ATs forget the first two letters; they won't stick with their partners through a bad patch, but go off and find a new one. Too late they then rediscover that they really *are* pretty 'connected' to their original partner, and get the two relationships all muddled up. As ATs don't think it's cool to be jealous, things don't get properly sorted out. The consequences: people ending up living in triangles, lots of stepchildren. One way through is the collective house and a system of polyfidelity.

Bringing up baby

These rites of passage often indicate an imminent desire to produce. This is known as 'playing mummies and daddies' (shows you have been in therapy).

The first stage in this elaborate process (after getting pregnant, that is; not difficult if you practise natural birth control), is getting the right baby books. These are:

Anything by Sheila Kitzinger
Magical Child by Joseph Chilton Pearce
Birth Without Violence by Frederick Leboyer
Birth Reborn by Michel Odent
The Whole Birth Catalog
Spiritual Midwifery by Ina May Gaskin
The New Age Childcare Book by Ann Wigmore
T.A. for Tots by Alwyn Freed (helps parents and children get along together)

During pregnancy, attendance at 'yoga and pregnancy' classes is *de rigeur*, as is the taking of a homeopathic medicine course and the consumption of biological food supplements (these look like tomato plant feed but are very good). 'Squaw Root' should be taken just before the birth to prepare the uterus for labour, and burdock if there is a tendency to miscarry. Raspberry leaf tea is good, too. Birth at home is preferable but hospitals in some parts of the country do now supply birthing chairs, bolsters etc., and the Leboyer method is popular. Those who are right up to date go for Michel Odent's *Active Birth* methods. Although possible to do in hospital, even better is to get hold of a radical midwife for the home birth. Sip 'rescue remedy' during labour; the father should be present to support his partner during contractions (active birth involves giving birth in a squatting position) and providing supplies of Arnica. Eat the afterbirth and get rid of those postnatal blues. AT's fry it up with chopped onions. Breastfeeding should be extended for far longer than was considered correct a decade or two ago – eighteen months is about the minimum.

Breastfeed, whenever possible, *in public* (a particularly good spot is the local bus station). AT mothers breastfeed each other's children. Introducing the child to vegetarian food right at the start is quite okay and there are good 'vegetarian food for babies' books around to help.

Dirt is good for kids to eat, traditionally a major source of vitamin B_{12} in vegan communities. Potty training is not something AT parents pursue with any great vigour. They don't want their child joining the army or the Conservative Party when he/she grows up. ATs don't use a pram, they always carry the baby in a canvas sling, Bolivian-style. AT parents believe in their children expressing all emotions, e.g., eight- to eighteen-year-olds are free to hit other children with bricks of natural wood, because bottling up one's feelings in childhood leads to problems in later life. Children who bash AT kids are, of course, already disturbed. AT parents do not believe in children's bedtimes; the children must decide for themselves. This is sometimes overruled at midnight if parents want to go to bed and their two-year-olds don't.

When out, it's very bad form to hold children's hands; much better to let them trail behind, or hold on to mother's long skirt.

Children's books

Your children's bookshelf should have the following on it to show that you're bringing them up the 'AT way'.

Lots of gnome literature – fantasy is in
Grimms' *Fairy Tales*
Andrew Lang's fairy tale books

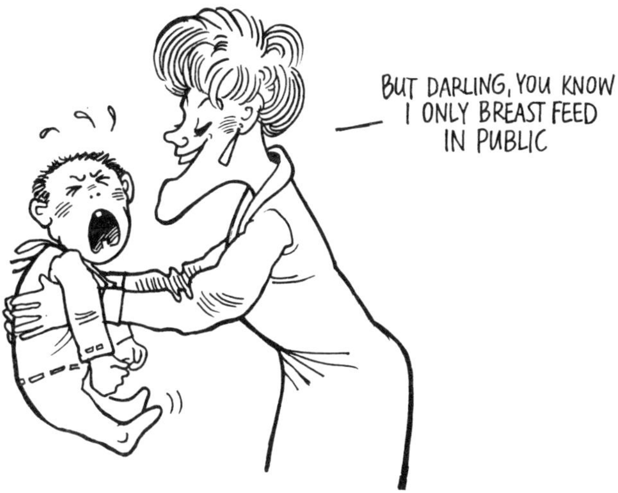

Where the Wild Things Are: Maurice Sendak
Animal literature (remember the hare as the carrier of new life)
The Hobbit: J. R. R. Tolkien
C. S. Lewis books
Arthur Ransome books
Lewis Carroll's 'Alice' books
The Little Prince: Saint-Exupery
Lots of Red Indian books (but be careful they don't give negative ethnic stereotypes)
Dr Seuss books (*The Butter Battle Book* is popular at the moment)
Right-on non-sexist books with titles like *Thomas Bakes a Cake* or *Emily the Engine Driver*
Sharing Nature with Children: Joseph Bharat Cornell (exercises include covering your nine-year-old in leaves and other woodland garbage and leaving her to be absolutely immobile until wild creatures come out and start walking over her – for direct experience of nature).

Naming your child

The kinds of names other people give their children are quite unsuitable: Kelly, Wayne, Craig, Darren, Jason, Scott, Tracy imply you watch too much popular television.

Rupert, Humphrey, Charlotte, Diana, Jasper are for the jet set, but the *principle* there is worth adopting; they are easily recognizable as such, everyone *knows* you've got a pile or a title (or both) with a name like that, so get your children off to a good start in life with an AT name. Your child's name should relate to an interest/obsession on your part, whether it be herbal, mystical, ethnic (perhaps a 'souvenir' of that trip around Africa or to the East), the name of the hero/heroine in your favourite (right-on) novel, or as a last resort, just plain obscure will do – at least they'll stand out in a crowd.

Herbal: Yarrow, Thyme, Saffron, Coriander, Tamarind
Mystical: Inanna (the queen of heaven and earth in Sumerian mythology – extra point for non-European mythology)
Ethnic: Illundi ('love child' in an Angolan tribe's dialect)
Jegeg ('pretty' in Balinese)
Tamar (Hebrew for 'date palm')
Zenzila ('Gift from above' in Xhosa)
Novels: Metzger (*The Crying of Lot 49*)
Yossarian (*Catch-22*)

Old-fashioned names: for girls, Rosie, Maisie, Martha, Adelaide; for boys, Sam, Tom, Jack, Nathan.

The counterculture has produced its own special crop, too:

Tree
Leaf
Fern
Willow
Earth (or for the very chic, Terre)
Sky
Reality
China (a bit dated, now that the counter revolution has set in)
Rainbow

Androgynous names are making a come-back:

Hilary
Vivian
Lindsay
Gabriel

Keep ahead of the crowd, a name for the future:

Gaia

A Girl Called Tractor

The Soviet trade union paper *Trud* reported at the end of 1984 that Russian children given names like 'Tractor' or 'Electricity' by their parents, in honour of the advances made in collective agriculture under Stalin, are now officially permitted 'to change them to something less embarrassing'.

The use of names in this way is by no means confined to our own culture or era (see boxes).

Some people who haven't quite the nerve to saddle their children for life with these names give them to their pets instead – cats are particularly liable to such treatment – and show off intellectual one-up membership at the same time, e.g.:

Collette	Suzy Q
Minnaloushe (from Yeats)	Hercules
Padmasambhava	Balzac
Wo fat	Zola
Trillo (celtic saint)	Mao
Heathcliffe	

Dogs don't seem to come in for quite the same treatment, perhaps because their owners would get embarrassed shouting their names across the local park. Nevertheless some do get ancient Greek names like Dido or Psyche, or even Medea.

The counterculture and the rise of feminism have produced a potent brew when it comes to people's surnames. Throwing off your inherited surname is all the rage. It started in the sixties with names like Salli Raspberry and Susie Creemcheese, but things have moved on quite a bit and these names seem rather dated now. The 1980s versions include:

Sunchild	Stillwater
Stonechild	Rainwater
Rainbow	Runwater
Sunshine	Solstice
Moondaughter	

Or for those that were more explicitly reject patriarchal names, Smith, Jones or Brown becomes:

Motherson	Solo
Freeborn	Joycechild
Human	Mariechild
Only	

Particular sects go in for name changes, too. Thus surnames like Heartfelt, Riches or Breathe indicate rebirthers.

By their names shall ye know them

Earlier this century a New England couple, Victor and Lilian Rostow, had two sons. The elder, born in 1913, they christened Eugene Debs Rostow in honour of America's best known socialist, politician and writer Eugene Debs. The second, born in 1916, they named Walt Whitman Rostow after the well known Utopian poet, visionary and gay activist, Walt Whitman. The sons of this idealistic and progressive New England couple have now grown up, and indeed become rather famous, but not, perhaps, quite as their parents intended:

'Walt' Rostow grew up to become an economist and economic historian and has been one of the leading intellectual advocates of the 'Pax Americana' policy of economic domination of the world economy, serving stints on the Inter-American Committee for the Alliance for Progress in the mid-1960s and as 'special assistant to the President' in the late 1960s. Meanwhile his elder brother 'Gene' Rostow was president of the Atlantic Treaty Association in 1973, the organization dedicated to the strengthening of NATO; from 1976 to 1981 he was chairman of the Executive Committee of 'The Committee on the Present Danger' (i.e. the Russians); and in 1981 newly elected President Ronald Reagan appointed him director of his Arms Control and Disarmament Agency – with a brief to do the opposite.

Education

Education starts young. Little ATs should be in playschool by three at the latest. Those whose parents go out to work find themselves in creches a lot earlier (preferably run by your right-on AT men's creche group). These days it's possible to select a toddler playschool reflecting AT values – and education is extremely high up on the list of priorities. Activities and their goals are itemized. Thus one school starts with: 'Greeting children and parents', the goals of which are explained as attempting to foster 'self-esteem, health, awareness, personal relationships, comfort, and a good start to the day'. Quite a lot from the simple phrase, 'Good morning'.

In towns ATs often take their babies along to 'Mother and Toddler' groups. This offers one of those rare encounters with working-class parents (mothers), in the process confirming the conviction that ATs *do* know best.

Grandparents and other relatives can be a problem, too. They have a tendency to give AT children very unsuitable toys and other presents at Christmas and birthdays. Right-on AT parents make many of their children's toys themselves – out of natural materials, as simple and unbreakable as possible. Others can be suitably modified. Thus Action Man kits (a less suitable present can hardly be imagined) can be modified by disposing of the clothes and other gear, and redressing the doll in miniaturized AT-style clothing to produce 'Direct-action

Man' (or Woman) – complete, for the very conscientious parent, with miniature wire-clippers.

As they grow older, full-time schooling of some sort becomes an issue. A lot of ATs support the state system, and indeed can be great advocates of it, though they recognize its deficiencies and are eager to improve it. Some find the competitive and materialistic values it inculcates too much, and keep their children home. The organization Education Otherwise has grown out of this trend. It acts as a support group for AT parents, but most of those who keep their children out of school are so individualistic that they don't cooperate with fellow parents to set up any alternative. Many, however, think and *talk* about starting their own school. Sometimes they dump their children on their local Woodcraft Folk group (a kind of AT alternative to scouts

and guides, and largely confined to towns) where the little darlings are readily identified as the most disruptive, poorly socialized and selfish members of the group (not the children's fault).

Parents with a more philosophical basis to their beliefs sometimes opt for Waldorf schools. These are run on the anthroposophical principles of Rudolph Steiner, but are thinly scattered (only about twenty in the UK). Named after the Waldorf-Astoria cigarette factory in Stuttgart where the first school was founded for the workers by Steiner in 1919, Steiner education is grounded in the recognition of both the physical and spiritual aspects of children, and espouses a three-fold nature of human beings: the willing, the feeling and the thinking. Thus for little children emphasis is on the education of the will, the impulse to do things: modelling, gardening, handwork, painting, songs and games, cooking and eurythmy (an art of movement to music and speech) and free play are its basis. Anthroposophists go for painting without clear form (wet paper), and strange-shaped buildings (no corners or rectangles if possible). Women wear long wool skirts; men wear unbuttoned check shirts over roll-necked jerseys.

Others go for Montessori schools and nurseries for 'non-directed' learning. ATs with the money send (or used to) their children to Dartington Hall. However with fees at £6000 a year, numbers are restricted. A. S. Neill of Summerhill is still spoken of in reverential terms by ATs discussing education.

Lifestyle

The House

You don't *have* to live in a house. Living on a narrow boat is very AT. So is living in a circus showman's caravan, and living in a tipi or 'bender'*, if uncomfortable, will certainly be a conversation topic at parties. Everyone aspires to 'living in the country' in a large house, with several acres for goats, bees, vegetables, orchard, lots of room for the children to play, and plentiful outbuildings – possibilities for conversion into a space for running your own therapy groups, a

* Originally gypsy houses built from a framework of bent hazel sticks, more elaborate than those at Greenham Common, with old carpets and tarpaulins, rather than sheets of plastic, for the roof.

Home sweet home – but you don't have to live in a house

meditation room perhaps, or even, for the more ambitious, a small private exhibition room/art gallery/craft room. Energy efficiency is a touchstone: insulation in the loft, solar panels on the roof, and, for the very adventurous, a windmill in the orchard. All this costs a lot of money (even in the south west) so collective living is certainly one way round it (you can talk knowingly about 're-creating the extended family'), and it explains those copies of *Country Life* in your living room to the sceptical right-on visitor ('We are looking for a collective house in the country'). An interesting development along these lines is the growing move to the country among separatist feminists, who create women-only land and build a life where they don't have to engage with men at all. Meantime it's multi-occupation (or, for the slightly better off, the-nuclear-family-plus-lodger) in the anytown muesli belt.

The-nuclear-family-plus-lodger

The semi-detached tipi

House names

In towns the number will do. They should be French provincial blue and white enamel on the scrubbed pine door. In the country you go for something that will ensure visitors know they have found the right place when they arrive, like:

Middle Earth (Tolkien fans)
Walden (Utopians)
Middle Way } (Buddhists)
Mount Meru }
Beltane House (Goddess worshippers)
Gaia House (Pseud)
Greenpeace

(that is if they haven't noticed the anti-nuke, rainbow and endangered species stickers already)

The Kitchen

The kitchen is the centre of the house. A good kitchen should have an Aga or Rayburn. Failing that, the cooker should be gas *not* electricity. (Electricity, like plastic, is very non-AT and should be kept where it belongs – powering lights and hi-fi equipment.)

The anti-plastic drive should even extend to a wooden plate rack, though of course in time it will warp. Shelves should line the walls with massive jars containing rice (brown), lentils (green, red and brown), split peas, beans (the more varieties the better), grains (red, green and brown) and dried fruit. Ideally they should be the heavy glass ones with cork lids, but a higgledy-piggledy mix of different shapes and sizes has a certain ethnic charm. Avoid the ones which have 'rice', 'lentils', 'flour' etc. written on them – you'll never get the right item in the right jar. A wide selection of herbs and spices on shelves above the Aga are a must. These can be labelled (mistaking the chilli for paprika could be disastrous), though it's much cooler not to – it proves you can identify them all by smell and leaf formation. Garlic and shallots should be on a long string, and supplies of fresh herbs are a good idea too (as you grow your own). Don't go in for designer kitchens or kitchenware (Habitat is out). Coffee-mills inherited from your grandparents, ancient weighing scales bought at the closing-down sale of a rural Co-op store, salad bowls and serving spoons brought back from your six months' meditation course in Sri Lanka, old-looking-cottage hand-knitted tea-cosies are much more your line. Pine is in, so are bright colours (repaint the fridge red). Design and build all the kitchen cupboards yourself and don't get obsessive about colour coordination, or a professional finish on them. Leave plenty of space for the

five-litre can of sunflower oil
sack of potatoes
sack of organic brown flour
compost bucket
bin for fermenting home brew in (and the bottles)
large bread crock
Ambig seed sprouter

Kitchen equipment should include a wok (you got it years before the multiples got on to them), enormous heavy cast-iron skillets, cast-iron and earthenware pots of all shapes and sizes, a mixer/blender (your one concession to modernity), a couple of large chopping boards, baking tins, and a large jar containing all those bits and pieces that don't seem to fit anywhere else – garlic crusher, whisks, spatulas, wooden spoons, a screwdriver and other stray carpentry tools (construction is an on-going process, and plenty of sharp knives (Japanese, or a French 'Opinel' pocket knife – scratch the varnish off the handle and rub it with oil). Also kitchen graffiti board. Wooden plates and bowls are a good thing (they don't break when the kids throw them on the floor), or lots of different china plates from junk shops (never sets of things which match). Drink from mugs, not cups (you made some of them yourself). 'Best' cutlery is a set of (genuine Chinese) chopsticks ('best' crockery likewise).

Part of the shelves is reserved for cookbooks. These should be:

The Friends of the Earth Cook Book
The Tassajara Bread Book
Mollie Kantzen: *The Moosewood Cook Book* (better still its sequel, *The Enchanted Broccoli Forest*)
Francis Moore Lappé: *Diet for a Small Planet*
Richard Mabey: *Food for Free*
Michel Abeshon: *Zen Macrobiotic Cooking*
Joy Larcom: *Salads the Year Round*
Alan Gear: *The Organic Food Guide*
The Book of Tofu
Culpepper's Herbal
Rose Elliot's *The Bean Book*

The kitchen should be big enough to include the dining table (stripped pine) and a Welsh dresser (ditto) for hanging mugs, storing plates, cheeseboard, fruit bowl and things that get damaged, toys, pet food, torches, road maps, and five-year-old camping guides. Hanging plants in season. Dining chairs should be wood for preference, but should not look as if they are part of the 'set' with the table.

The AT kitchen has a large larder, well stocked with home-made jams (the only acceptable way of consuming sugar), marmalades, home-made honey, free-range eggs, and pickles and preserves of all sorts (including such unlikely delicacies as pickled unripe walnuts), in large kilner jars. Top score for the pre-1948 variety. ATs, you see, don't have freezers. The large quantities of home brew are to be found in here too.

The Living Room

Avoid the 'place for everything and everything in its place' look (shouldn't be difficult, especially with children). If the living room is reserved for 'grown-ups' (what are they?), it should have a sanded and polished pine floor with colourful ethnic rugs brought back from foreign trips. Otherwise, wall-to-wall industrial carpeting – grey. A woodburning stove in the fireplace should be the centrepiece of the room, with a large wicker basket beside it full of *dry* wood, and there should be an all-pervading smell of woodsmoke which has replaced the joss sticks and patchouli oil as the smell of the 1980s. Furniture should be rolled-up futons (can be unrolled to sleep guests when necessary), large cushions, and a large sofa covered in natural fibres – wool, flannel, tweed or canvas are good fabrics. Bookshelves should line one wall (but don't go overboard, nobody wants to live in a library). These should contain the required list (see page 62) to which you are allowed to add:

Books left over from your university degree (if you did one)
Maps and guides
Baby books (see reading list)
Back issues of magazines (ditto)
Books on your special interest(s) (buddhism, natural health, organic gardening, psychotherapy, feminist sci-fi)
Some reference books
Books on home energy conservation, e.g. *Radical Technology* and well-thumbed copies of books like *Self-help House Repairs* (from your 'squatting' past)
Books on wild flowers, rocks, trees, birds, seaweed etc. (standardized format)
Books written by your friends

A desk in the corner is acceptable. Letters from AT friends are recognizable by their handwriting – using black ink and a thick nib, they circle rather than dot their i's. Flowers abound. ATs are often left-handed – proves they have a dominant 'right brain'. Envelopes will be encrusted with re-use stickers, and slogans like 'Help create cloud cuckoo land on earth'.

A reasonable music centre and supply of records and tapes are essential, but not too flashy unless a professional musician. Ideally a piano should fit in somewhere (if the kids have a playroom it *could* go in there), as well as a guitar and other musical instruments on the walls, especially ethnic-looking drums and flute-type instruments that nobody can get a note out of. Coffee table (made by a friend, with hand-glazed tiles on top) should have the magazines *Resurgence, New Internationalist* and *Country Life* and one or two 'alternative coffee table books' (current favourites: *The Gaia Atlas of Planet Management* and *The Body Shop Book*). Plenty of flowers, cut from the garden, and in pots. In winter, dried flowers. You can tell they're

Balansing act

The Balans chair, an ungainly looking contraption with no back or legs, just a place to tuck your knees, is likely to become the 'earth shoe' of the 1980s. Some say it was invented by Norwegian architects, others by US doctors for the wounded of World War II. Certainly this ingenious seating device has been around for at least thirty years. President Mitterrand is a fan; he has his own miniature chrome model. The manufacturers insist that the chair relieves musculoskeletal stress by distributing body weight evenly between knees and back. The man who designed Mitterrand's version claims that Balans chairs will eventually account for over 30 per cent of all the world's seating. Balans also created the 'Tripp Trapp' chair. Used as a high chair, the level of seat- and foot-rest can be adjusted, and it doesn't tip up when used to stand on for changing light-bulbs.

mostly middle class (definition of a middle-class household: 'furniture in the garden – flowers in the house'). A TV is okay, but better in the playroom. Same with the computer which is mostly used by the children, but challenging the computer to chess is allowed. Ornaments should include something exotic: a gorilla skull in a glass case is excellent ('My grandmother picked it up at a Liberal Party fete for five shillings'); inexpensive souvenirs from distant travels (nothing tacky); a piece of modern art if you can afford it (or better still, know the artist) or if not, framed pictures by your under-five-year-old children. Lighting should be subdued – none of this trendy track lighting, though one spotlight is okay. Walls should be painted in light colours but *not* brilliant white. Light-coloured walls allow pictures, photographs, wall-hangings and other ornaments to be shown off to best advantage.

AT Guide to Estate Agents' Jargon

So you've finally decided to take the plunge and move to the country. Here's a guide to the estate agent's jargon and what it all means:

Some quite magnificent rural views – *other views are of a power station and an oil refinery*
Virtually detached – *on the edge of a cliff*
Situated right in the heart of the village – *pub with erratic closing times next door*
Mainly lawned garden – *garden has not been tended for years*
Cottage enjoys a lovely rural location – *bus route axed in the 1950s*
Enjoying almost timeless environment – *buses never ran anywhere near it*
Property rethatched in recent years – *roof fell in recently*
Cottage dating some 300 years with tremendous amount of character – *no electricity or running water*
Roomy accommodation – *two rooms*
Outside laundry – *stream nearby*
Easily managed garden } *garden even smaller than the house*
Delightful cottage garden }
Useful range of outbuildings – *ruined shed*
Unique – *unmortgageable*

Retains many original features – *roof leaks*
A wealth of traditional features – *roof leaks and drains blocked*
Mentioned in the Domesday book – *has a plague pit in the garden*
Two attractive fireplaces – *no other form of heating*
A wealth of beams – *deathwatch beetle infestation*
Suitable for further updating – *in need of complete renovation*
A worthy and ideal subject for modernization – *dangerous structure notice served*
Skilfully extended – *DIY job*
Thatched barn has consent to convert to self-contained granny annexe – *sorry we have just doubled the price*

The Bathroom and Bedroom

The bathroom should have shower (or at least shower attachment) as well as bath, colourful blinds, large mirror, shells, potted plants, recycled loo paper, anti-nuke posters on back of door, jerrycan with funnel for collecting pee for organic compost activator, wooden loo seat and loo roll-holder. Also necessary: impressive collection of alternative skin care and other beauty products, seaweed shampoo, honey and almond moisturizer, cedarwood handcream, bergamot suntan oil, calendula ointment, comfrey and yarrow cleanser, elderflower hair gel . . . that kind of thing. None, of course, should have been tested on animals.

Bedroom: keep it simple. Futon (the waterbed, symbol of the 1960s, is out), duvet, ethnic or handmade patchwork quilt, chest of drawers with flowers on, big paper globe lampshade. If space allows, the bed should be on a raised platform with winding staircase, perilously loaded with candles and dusty books (Anaïs Nin erotica, Stevie Smith poems – sex manuals are out), incense sticks, plastic oyster, and speculum left out from self-exam group, briefly enjoyed but now abandoned.

Books

Books are an important part of an AT lifestyle. When coming into your house for the first time, visitors will often scan your bookshelves to check you out. It's important to make the right impression. Books on New Age therapy, earth mysteries, the goddess, anything with Zen, Buddha or Tao in the title, New Age economics, organic gardening/self-sufficiency, feminist sci-fi and expanded consciousness books like those by Castaneda all score well. Here's a partial list (they are not divided into fiction and non-fiction categories as some people's fiction is other people's fact these days):

The I Ching
The Gnostic Gospels
The Tibetan Book of the Dead
Krishnamurti's journals
Anything by Carlos Castaneda
The Making of a Counter Culture or *Person/Planet:* Theodore Roszak
Zen and the Art of Motorcycle Maintenance: Robert Pirsig (still a classic)
Whole Earth Catalog (historic document, difficult to get hold of *Next Whole Earth Catalog* will do)
The Dispossessed: Ursula Leguin
Gravity's Rainbow: Thomas Pynchon
Woman and Nature: Susan Griffin
Woman on the Edge of Time: Marge Piercy
Michael Dames's books on Avebury, Silbury and the goddess

The Old Straight Track: Alfred Watkins (the original book on ley lines)
Any of the self-sufficiency books by John Seymour
If You Meet the Buddha on the Road, Kill Him!: Sheldon Kopp
The Tao of Pooh: Benjamin Hoff
The Tao of Physics: Fritjof Capra
The Turning Point: Fritjof Capra
Gaia: a New Look at Life on Earth: James Lovelock
The Gaia Atlas of Planet Management: Norman Myers (ed.)
The Dancing Wu Li Masters: Gary Zukav
Small is Beautiful: E. F. Schumacher (the bible)
The Lord of the Rings: J. R. R. Tolkien
The Politics of Experience and The Bird of Paradise: R. D. Laing
Touch the Earth: T. C. McLuhan (ed.)
News from Nowhere: William Morris
The Glass Bead Game: Herman Hesse
Meetings with Remarkable Men: G. I. Gurdjieff
The Undiscovered Self: C. G. Jung
Walden: Henry David Thoreau
On Death and Dying: Elizabeth Kubler-Ross
Cutting through Spiritual Materialism: Chogyam Trungpa
Tools for Conviviality: Ivan Illich (other Illich books are good, too)
Creating Alternative Futures: Hazel Henderson
Entropy: a New World View: Jeremy Rifkind and Ted Howard

Mind and Nature: Gregory Bateson
From Red to Green: Rudolf Bahro
The Spirit of the Valley: Sukie Colegrave (combines Eastern mysticism with Jungian psychology, two AT interests)
Poetry by e. e. cummings
The Prophet: Kahlil Gibran (the Patience Strong of the alternative movement)
Supernature, or others by Lyall Watson
Autobiography of a Yogi: Yogananda
The Rocking of the Cradle and the Ruling of the World: Dorothy Dinnerstein
Richard's Bicycle Book
When the Wind Blows: Raymond Briggs
The Crack in the Cosmic Egg: Joseph Chilton Pearce
Programming and Meta-programming in the Human Biocomputer: John C. Lilley (for the title)

Magazines

Much that is important in the new age has yet to be published in books, though a few publishers, especially in the United States, are climbing on the bandwagon, notably Bantam Books with their 'New Age Books' imprint promoted in typically syrupy style as 'a search for meaning, growth and change'. Whether you'll find any of those things in them is debatable, but meanwhile magazines are an important way of spreading the message. You should have at least a few of the following prominently displayed:

Resurgence
New Age Journal (American trendsetter, very good)
Co-evolution Quarterly (it comes from Marin County so it's bang up to date)

Often these magazines have a short life, so back issues of the following show you've been keeping up with developments as they happened:

Undercurrents
Anarchy (when it was edited by Colin Ward, i.e. pre-1970)

Vole (especially the earlier editions with the glossy covers)
Tomorrow (politico-eco-fashion magazine bankrolled by fashion star Katharine Hamnett; only lasted one issue – keep it as a collector's item)

For the specialist:

Greenline (if interested in politics)
Human Potential Resources (for the Human Potential Movement)
New Humanity ('the world's first politico-spiritual journal')
Down by the Riverside (Buddhist)
One Earth (from the Findhorn Foundation)
Home Farm (previously called *Practical Self-sufficiency*)
The Friend (Quaker weekly journal)

Food and drink

The AT is vegetarian but not vegan. What the AT eats is really quite a contentious area, with desire and guilt coming into play in the collective conscience and causing rapid fluctuations in allegiance to one point of view or another.

Basically ATs are likely to be relatively recent converts to vegetarianism, and quite a few still have a hankering after meat. This explains the rapid increase in the demand for organically reared meat in the past few years – having your steak and eating it, so to speak. ATs have often experimented with the more complicated forms of diet – vegan, macrobiotic – and may even have been on one of those ten-day rice-only diets to cleanse the body of impurities, but in general they settle for vegetarianism (strictly lacto-vegetarianism) with all the conflicts and contradictions (such as eating fish; and the household hen that has ceased laying can also find its way into the pot – 'Well, it had a happy life'). The occasional hare, rabbit or pigeon from a local poacher is also an allowable exception. These days wholefoods have been superseded. It's 'gourmet natural foods', imported from the furthest corners of the globe (sorry, planet). The kind of thing now available includes:

- organic sausages (retailed at over £1 each, the pig has never seen a steroid or antibiotic)

- rennet-free Cornish nettle cheese at £2+ per pound (note: picked from the wildest spots in Cornwall, none of yer actual council tip nettles used)
- Essene seed bread (no flour or yeast). The recipe comes from a first-century Aramaic manuscript, 'The Essene Gospel of Peace'. It's made from the crushed sprouted seeds of organically grown wheat, sunflower, sesame, poppy, flax and caraway plants and is popular with those suffering from 'Candida', or yeast infection, this year's 'hot' disease.

Ideologically correct food is sometimes attempted. Avoid South African food of all kinds (especially fruit), go for Nicaragua or 'Campaign' (Tanzanian) coffee. Chilean onions were 'out' for a while.

The AT Dinner Party Menu

Inviting ATs to dinner can be a fraught affair these days. Vegetarian food? They've probably just become vegan. Milk? Eggs? Cheese? Coffee? Allergic reactions. True believers attempt to 'eliminate the toxins' by complicated rotations of foods, today 'goosefoots' (beet, spinach, swiss chard), tomorrow the nightshades (potato, tomato, aubergine, peppers). Woe betide you if you serve up the wrong veg. on the wrong day. If you're not completely fazed by all this you probably will be by the array of pills and medicines produced before and after the meal by the cognoscenti. For the more amenable, though, try this menu:

START WITH:
Sorrel or nettle soup (Free Food)

MAIN COURSE:
Any type of bean casserole with the liquid flavoured with tahini, tamari or tofu.

ACCOMPANIED BY:
Salad, which should include fresh herbs, dandelion and Lamb's lettuce leaves in season and a wide range of vegetables, all home-grown and organic if possible.

DESSERT:
Apple, rhubarb or blackberry wholemeal crumble with yoghourt. If it's a birthday or other celebration, follow main meal with a carob cake with handmade rainbow candle atop.

DRINK:
Be generous with the half gallon jug of last year's homemade elderflower wine.

Accompany by grain coffee, or peppermint tea. Irish whiskey or Polish vodka, if available, can be served if guests are still sober enough to accept.

'The Designer Bean'

The soya bean has for many years been recognized as an important source of protein. In Japan it's known as 'the meat of the fields'. Selling beans, however, even to vegetarians, isn't easy. Until now, that is: enter The Designer Bean. *The Book of Tofu* started it off in the USA and Western Europe and now the humble soya bean has been transformed into a score of new products to tempt the vegetarian palate. Not all of these are available in Britain yet, but it's best to stay ahead of the pack, talk about them knowingly before they arrive, and not be intimidated by them when they do.

The basic soya bean products are:
- tofu (soya bean curd, looks a little like solid cream cheese)
- miso (fermented soya bean paste)
- tempeh (see below)
- tamari (soya sauce)

From the bean you get:
- soynut (like peanuts)
- soy flour (for making anything from bread and doughnuts to pizza bases and ravioli)
- soy milk and its offshoot, soy sorbet/ice cream (known to afficionados as 'ice-bean') now available in right-on flavours, such as carob and hazel nut.

From tofu:
- carob pemmican (like a trail food bar)
- vegi dips
- soyannaise
- tofu sausage
- tofu burgers
- tofu cheesecake

From miso:
- miso cup (broth)
- miso soup
- miso mustard (includes barley)
- beenut butter (miso blended with peanuts, honey and bee pollen)

Tempeh is Indonesian in origin, lightly cooked, hulled soya beans cultured in a mould – tastes a bit like a cross between chicken and mushrooms.

Drink

Purity is in, stimulants are out. Pure bottled carbonated spring water extracted from some appropriate beauty spot is increasingly popular. Dreadfully expensive for plain water. It must be something to do with the claims on the label: 'The natural alternative – calorie free' (unlike the horrid fattening stuff you get from taps). On a hot day what better to drop into a glass of this nectar than 2000-year-old glacial ice hacked from the glaciers of Antarctica and guaranteed no impurities (if you believe that you'll believe anything).

For a chilly winter evening the range of warming, non-stimulant drinks is quite extensive these days. There's been a revival among ATs drinking beverages more familiar to our great-grandparents than present generations, such as:

dandelion coffee
limeflower
elderflower
vervain
hibiscus
camomile
and rosehip teas
as well as barley cup (made from barley, a coffee substitute)
carob cup (like barley cup but made from carob beans – the AT's 'hot chocolate')

postum (upmarket barley cup)
grain coffee (made from grain, no coffee beans in it)

When fellow ATs drop by, barley cup or carob cup with plant milk is a good hospitality drink. *Never* offer real coffee, not even de-caff. If you must drink milk, stick to the green top variety (unpasteurized).

The new demand for herbal teas has spawned all sorts of combinations of variable quality. The meditatively inclined go for three-year-old Bancha tea from Japan (used to keep you awake during meditation). Some claim a political impulse. As the promo for one says: 'When things get "hot" on the nuclear scene and your own cooling system is about to melt down, it's time for a cup of "nuclear casual tea".' (Get it?) Ideal for that weekend occupation of a nuclear reactor site, its ingredients include rose petals and buds, camomile flowers, hop leaves, catnip leaves, spearmint leaves and rosemary leaves. Another popular line has been the Celestial Seasonings herb teas, regaling in such delightful names as 'sleepy time', 'mandarin orange spice' and 'red zinger'. The packets used to be covered with little pieces of homespun wisdom, but they became too successful and were taken over. Now they are the corporate cousins of Tupperware!* Any self-respecting AT will clear their cupboard of them right away on hearing this news.

* Actually of everything from Kraft cheese or Duracell batteries, a small part of one of America's 'top 30' companies Dart-Kraft.

Alcohol is quite okay. Home brew is definitely best – beer or wine (especially elderflower, parsnip, dandelion or oak leaf) in pretty large quantities at festival times. Home-brewed lager is for wallies. Spirits can't be made at home so easily, so the AT usually survives on erratic supplies of duty-free from trips abroad. Current favourites:

Jameson's Irish whiskey
Polish vodka
American rye bourbon

Drugs aren't a big deal, the ATs get 'natural highs' from their connectedness with the earth and the spirit. However it is allowed to help the process along with a little grass (home-grown), sinsemilla* or hash when available, and a small stock of magic mushrooms picked locally in the autumn (most get consumed fresh, which is the best way, but a few are dried and stored for high days and holidays). Souvenirs from foreign trips – coca leaves, mescalin, perhaps a little 'moroccan' – are allowable (all natural highs, of course). Glue and even acid are out, and so are 'designer drugs' like MDA, 'Extacy' and MDMA (the 'love drug'). A lot of ATs have given up smoking, but if they still do it, they roll their own, very thin, using blue Rizla or liquorice paper (the thinnest, to use up less trees) and distinctive pouch. Various herbal mixtures, or, ironically, Dutch aromatic tobacco (high tar), are now becoming more popular. Some AT households ban smoking indoors. Smokers are banished to the garden or allotment.

Dressing up

ATs are very clothes-conscious in an understated way. They don't like uniforms of the traditional kind, but have their own instead. Country ATs either make their own clothes, out of hardwearing no-nonsense natural fibres, or buy thick, prickly Welsh wool shirts which will last a lifetime.

Town ATs get a certain amount of clothing from jumble sales, but this is supplemented by things they make themselves and some items

* Developed in California (where else?), where it was discovered that by uprooting male cannabis plants, the female puts out richer and larger buds in a vain attempt at fertilization.

from Laura Ashley and Clothkits (for women), though they are careful not to get typecast (you don't want to be mistaken for someone who works for Channel 4, the Open University or the GLC!). Keep well away from 'designer' clothes, and anything advertised in the pages of colour supplements or glossy women's magazines.

Apart from these, the big no's are anything new – apart from hand-made, hand-dyed, hand-stitched or hand-knitted – or any man-made fibres. Wool is *the* material, preferably a little matted. Chic clothes for men are Fair Isle V-neck wool slipovers, and for women,

1930s and 1940s crepe dresses finishing around the knees, worn with brightly coloured thick tights and hand-knitted legwarmers, or long skirts from any third world country, and no bras. Any knitwear from South America is still in, also Afghan or Guatemalan embroidery, and

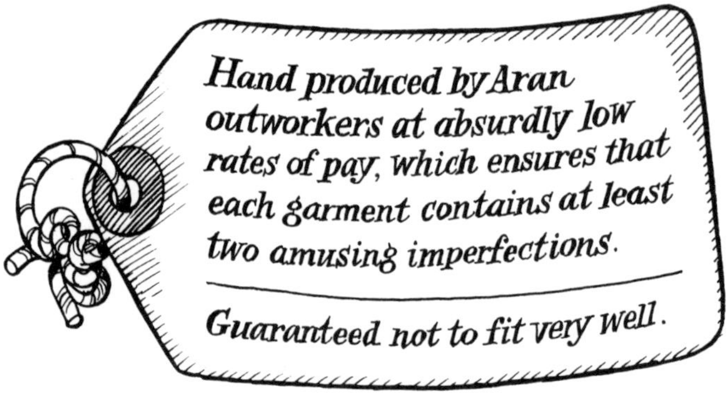

ethnic jewellery, brass or heavy silver with turquoise or large amber beads, souvenirs from distant travels. Silver anklets with little bells on them are worn by some AT women. Bulky hand-knitted jumpers in rainbow colours, or ethnic 'natural colours' with relevant symbols (e.g., magic mushrooms) incorporated into the pattern are good for both sexes.

Hairstyle: top fashion is long tousled/tangled fair hair.

Healers go for soft textures and pastel healing colours that suit the wearer. Wearing 'your' colour is very conscious. The 'New Age man' can be seen in pink and lemon-yellow looking a bit like a cross between Brooks brothers and Marx brothers. He looks best in plimsolls and baggy trousers. Bright stylish clothes are quite acceptable, especially Hamnett pants; men, in particular, are making up for centuries of regimentation. Keep an eye open for people with an unusually high proportion of reds, maroons and oranges in their wardrobe – a sign of a lapsed sanyasin (Bhagwan followers). The unconscious ambivalence of the past has been replaced by conscious ambiguity, androgynous clothing for both sexes is in.

Clothing and hairstyle are the areas where the 'punk/hippie generation gap' shows most clearly (politics is the other – punks are more into vegetarianism and animal rights). Younger ATs are influenced by post-punk fashion: Katharine Hamnett T-shirts with their enormous political slogans, way-out earrings and tinted and coloured hair are *de rigueur* for both sexes. However, some older ATs are now being subtly influenced by youth culture too. They sneak off and streak their hair, using setting gel to make it stand up, and are occasionally seen ostentatiously reading copies of *The Face*.

Badges are popular – needn't necessarily be political, self-deprecatory ones are now quite fashionable; things like: 'My analyst says I don't exist'.

AT purists don't wear watches. They are into body time. They get very confused when clocks go back or forward. AT homes are time-charted by wind-up and pendulum clocks. These are fiendishly expensive to maintain, but somehow it's possible to excuse a hand-wound clock if it skips the odd half hour. If a Taiwanese battery job malfunctions, ATs get very angry. For those who *do* wear watches, the old-fashioned sweep hand variety is the thing. Digital watches are out. ATs like to feel connected with the cyclical nature of time – the rising and setting of the sun, the passage of the seasons: digital watches destroy this cyclical nature, making it linear and chopping it up into little pieces.

Dungarees are for children only. OshKosh dungarees with carpenter's tools on them are very chic for little girls. For young

children chicest clothes for summer are wellies with no socks, worn with woollen vest and no knickers.

Footwear is still heavily influenced by the 1970s craze for the 'earth shoe'. Ethnic still rules. Earth shoes, birkenstocks (a form of sandal), clogs and, for the more fashion-conscious, hikers/kickers in bright colours. Bright-coloured hand-made shoes are very AT. Bright green is particularly popular. Anything that looks like a Cornish pasty is very suitable for either sex. Black 'monkey boots', pastel-shaded espadrilles and black Chinese slippers are popular with the female of the species. In the country bare feet are popular (in spite of the climate).

The garden

The AT garden will be organic. Nothing that destroys the natural cycles of the earth is allowed – no herbicides, pesticides, fungicides, chemical fertilizers or other agro-chemicals are allowed. This may well reduce your crops, at least in the early stages as you find out how it all works the hard way, but, as mothers used to say to their daughters, 'You have to suffer to be beautiful.' You'll soon pick up the 'in' phrases like:

companion planting	mulching
'no dig' gardening	raised beds
deep beds	permaculture

You may even get into the more recherché aspects of the organic movement like bio-dynamic gardening (developed by followers of Rudolph Steiner, involves planting seeds according to the cycles of the moon), or join the Henry Doubleday Research Association. You've 'arrived' when your garden or smallholding is officially approved as suitable for 'Wwoofers' (town-based ATs who escape to the country to 'work weekends on organic farms'). True ATs avoid the temptation to give their Wwoofers all the really dirty and difficult jobs, like grubbing up the ground elder or docks.

In the country, AT gardens are enormous, and should contain the following:

orchard (with several kinds of apple trees including cider-apples)
nutwalk (optional luxury)
goats
bees
hens (possibly 'rescued' from a factory farm – produce happy eggs)
ducks and geese
two pet lambs, which are allowed in the house
large areas of green manure (particularly comfrey)
large compost heaps (mulch-covered)
substantial herb garden (include basil, coriander, lovage and borage)

The geodesic greenhouse: ATs like to apply their alternative technology

large area for soft fruit (having an aged mulberry tree is also a great plus)
six-foot dope plant (because it looks nice)
fig trees and vines on south-facing walls
a greenhouse (large)
plenty of children's playspace (particularly important to have 'elemental' play area – sand, water etc.)
a gazebo (use it for storing apples, perhaps, or as a meditation room).

For the very lucky, running water somewhere in the garden; for those more contemplative moments – celestial music while you work. Those in such fortunate circumstances can grow whatever they like, but those stuck with a back garden and/or allotment in the muesli belt need to be much more selective, and time is often limited too. So selecting the right seeds from the right *catalogues* is most important.

The better catalogues offer a good read as well as a good seed. Here's a run-down on next summer's 'hot crops' – the chic greens and grains that the leading-edge AT is carrying, and carrying on, about:

- Amaranti (ancient super-protein miracle grain, which also comes in a vegetable variety boasting spinach-like leaves)
- Chinese okra (a.k.a. loofah – when young is an edible gourd; when older, the skeleton is the thing you use in the bath)
- Mache (Lamb's lettuce), radiccho, roequette (alias Argula) – salad greens in vogue with the gourmet food crowd
- Mitsuba (Japanese parsley – a bit like celery too)
- Miner's lettuce (a.k.a. winter purslane – the AT's little act of solidarity)
- Salsify (sometimes known as vegetable oyster – originates in Sandwich Islands)
- Scorzonera (long, black-skinned root, medieval origins)
- Shingiku (a chrysanthemum grown for its 'chop suey greens')

Other 'fun vegetables' popular this year included Egyptian walking onions (proliferate without replanting), elephant garlic (sometimes called Jumbo garlic in catalogues), and the child-pleasing 'vegetable spaghetti' gourd.

Gardener's 'Helpers'

Today all vegetables can easily take over your life, so take care. There is nothing sadder than the sight of an ex-AT turned into a self-sufficiency freak, a 'dawn to dusk materialist' whose entire life revolves round planting potatoes, digging them up and counting them, and who cannot talk about anything other than the size of the latest crop.

To help you avoid this sad end, here are some gardener's 'helpers' that make for organic gardening without (or with fewer) tears.

QR herbal compost hastener
Quassia chips (insecticide made from boiling the bark of a tree)
Sea magic (organic liquid spray based on seaweed)
Ferbsan slug killer (but harmless to hedgehogs, birds, pets etc.)

On wheels

ATs are into flexibility and economy on their means of transportation. Bicycles are a must. They come in two types. Old black ones with little white flowers lovingly painted on the frame, wicker baskets at the front, and hub dynamos operated by an electric light switch taped to the frame under the creaky leather saddle. These should have attachments for a bike trailer, the baby carrier and panniers. The alternative, for the serious biker, are the Claud Butler 10-speed. Light alloy, expensive (possibly the AT's most expensive possession), some have unisex 'mixte' frames. ATs with children sometimes have

THE BAMBOO CYCLE Co., Ltd., 59, Holborn Viaduct, London, E.C.

tricycles with back seats for kids in crash helmets. In towns cars aren't absolutely necessary, though most ATs have one, or at least access to one, through some complicated sharing arrangement. ATs only drive a limited range of vehicles. These are:

Renault 4s
Citroën 2 CVs or Dyanes
Morris Minor Estates (becoming something of a status symbol)
VW beetles with small screen pre-1960 (and no petrol gauge, use a dipstick instead – for people who practise natural birth control)
VW van (preferably split-screen model)
old van or ambulance, hand-painted with rainbows on the sides (maintained by AT specialists; not very good but you trust them)

Anything else is too big, too flashy, too expensive or too unrecognizable. The only *possible* exception is a certain kind of female therapist who drives a white MG sports car (she's feeling okay about the universe enriching her for her good work and feels justified in having good wheels to help her do more good work). All these cars soon adopt the personas of their owners. Most desirable colour is green (naturally), though white or sky blue are also okay. The sticker craze is particularly prevalent; the stickers to have are:

'Nuclear power no thanks' (preferably in Basque, Lappish, or at the very least Welsh)
CND or other peace sticker (white dove on blue background or 'Give peace a chance' rainbow are popular)
Something incorporating the sunflower symbol – symbol of the green movement.
Greenpeace 'Rainbow Warrior' sticker

An obscure 'nation' label – particularly prized are:

'Kernow' and 'Occitania'
'Ecosse' or 'Cymru' are okay
a clever slogan, e.g., 'The sun never sets on geothermal energy', 'One nuclear bomb can ruin your whole day', 'I brake for unicorns' or 'I'm sorry my karma has just run over your dogma'

ATs do *not* have stickers saying anything like:

- 'Windsurfers do it standing up' (or any other 'do it' stickers)
- 'My other car is a Porsche' (although 'my other car is a bicycle' just about gets into the 'clever slogan' category)
- or 'Preserve wild life – pickle a squirrel'

ATs aren't very good on cars. They know enough to change a wheel or replace the oil, some of them know how to use a set of jumpleads but that's about it.

A healthy compromise for the budding AT who can't cope with the ecological guilt of four wheels, but can't quite remember how to work the pedals, is a motorcycle. Any Japanese make is out; British, or Eastern European that leaks oil; is in. For top marks ride a Velocette or BSA C15, or MZ 250. Sidecars are making a come-back. Dress:

don't be seen in a leather jacket or full-face helmet with smoked visor. You need a faded Belstaff and an old peaked open face with glass goggles.

ATs are also very skilled at using trains cheaply, and know all the rules of rail cards. Children often come along to cheapen the adults' fares. A small subculture is developing in 'borrowing' other people's children to travel cheaply. ATs own their own BR timetable.

On holiday

It's not terribly classy for ATs to admit that they are going on holiday. Life is so meaningful you don't need one. Generally a break from it means visiting other ATs who live in an isolated unheated cottage/ community, or going on a camping trip (with Morris piled high) to Wales. March or October are favoured months. Nevertheless some ATs do go travelling in the summer (after all, the hippie trail to the East, or those six months on an Israeli kibbutz, were a crucial part of forming the AT identity in youth). Package holidays to Majorca or Tunisia, or, worst of all, going anywhere with Club Med, are absolutely out; instead, a new kind of holiday for the AT is now being created.

For the meditatively inclined, four weeks at an international meditation camp in the French Alps is a must ('experiencing something of what a hermit experiences in seclusion and retirement': you retire to a cave).

For those who prefer company on their holiday, the most fashionable Greek Island these days is Skyros in the Sporades. Home of the Skyros centre, a personal-growth summer community specializing in bio-energetics encounter, gestalt, massage and psycho-drama. Recently opened on the same island is the Atsitsa Club for those interested in the integration of the body, mind and spirit; yoga, tai chi, dream journeys and meditation are their speciality. All in all it's two weeks of sun, sea, sand and psycho-drama guaranteed.

Caribbean islands are now realizing the potential market too (so much more convenient for American customers). 'Macrobiotic Jamaica' is now on the menu. For the more adventurous still, there's:

- China by bicycle (in the old days it was study tours of the communes' agricultural system)
- Pilgrimage tours of Northern India and Nepal (for the really adventurous, visiting Buddhist monasteries around Mount Everest is now possible)
- Craft workshop tours of Nepal (including an 'optional week's extension for private tuition with a master craftsman of your choice')
- Visiting the Paro Festival of Bhutan

Or for those who can't let go:

- 'Acid Rain' expeditions in the High Sierras of California ('participants will conduct environmental studies . . . ')

Even the Pacific now caters for the new breed of holiday-maker. Why not visit the sacred stones of Rarotonga, Cook Islands, or go for a mystic journey under sail to the Galapagos, Hawaii or the islands off the coast of Alaska? ('Explore the healing power of the sea, visualize

and clarify your inner purpose and current life direction. Sailing experience not necessary.')

The ultimate, though, is surely two weeks visiting the Shamans and natural healers of Peru. Your group will have its own shaman attached to it for the duration who will make you his 'apprentices' when invoking the healing forces of ancient 'power centres', ceremonies that will involve 'ritual' drug-taking, and will lead participants through 'death ceremonies'. If you are ever likely to see Castanedas's 'crack between the world', this is the opportunity.

The kudos of having 'I have seen the natural healers of Peru' tags on your back-pack will make the ruinous expense all the more worthwhile.

For the rather less ambitious, home-grown opportunities abound too. Britain is scattered with ancient, sacred and mystical sites, and there's money to be made.

At the top end of the market, you can participate in a 'journey of attunement' round Britain's 'triangle of light' with no less a person than Findhorn founder, Peter Caddy. You'll visit Findhorn (naturally), Iona, Glastonbury and Stonehenge (I *know* most triangles don't have four points), tune into Arthurian legends, and attend a guest lecture from Sir George Trevelyan. Such spiritual tourism has a serious purpose. 'The tours seek to facilitate individual spiritual growth through understanding the Ancient Wisdom and the messages it has for us today,' says the facilitator of another brand.

Less goal-orientated and a lot cheaper, why not 'Head for the Hills'? Founded in the mid 1970s when 'head had more than one meaning', 'Head for the Hills' takes you walking in small groups to the wildest corners of Britain, along ancient trackways, past holy wells and sacred sites, sometimes ending up at events like the Elephant Fayre after a week crossing Dartmoor. Fed on vegetarian wholefoods, and staying in a magical camp which pops up ahead of you each evening, the idea is increasingly to tune into nature. The men on these walks can sometimes be heard enthusing about 'the female forms in the landscape', and finding ley lines is popular.

Popular culture

Music

The musical tastes of the AT can broadly be described as 'Country and Eastern'. Your collection should include a selection from the following:

- George Harrison
- Quintessence
- Incredible String Band (the early stuff, they went downhill after they got into scientology)
- Ry Cooder
- Van Morrison
- Leonard Cohen
- Bonzo Dog Band
- Arthur Brown
- Bob Dylan (early)
- The Roche Sisters
- John Lennon
- Pink Floyd
- Steve Hillage
- Vangelis
- Kitaro (ex-Bhagwan)
- Steven Halpern
- Cris Williamson (especially: 'The Changer and the Changed')
- Celtic music like Planxty and Clannad

The slightly more 'acid rock' types include:

- Frank Zappa
- The Doors
- Grace Slick/Grateful Dead
- Velvet Underground
- Laura Nyro

More recent stuff should include material emanating from the 'World Music' movement. Foremost among those is the Paul Winter Consort who started playing jazz and Eastern-influenced music before anyone else really thought of it. Their record 'Common Ground' included such unusual sidemen as an eagle, a wolf and a whale (though the whale was rumoured to be the same cetacean who sang on the Judy Collins album back in the early 1970s). Their recent record 'Callings' expands the orchestra of animal musicians to include seals, dolphins, otters, sea lions, beluga and a bowhead whale. James Galway and Brian Eno are 'in' and so is what is called 'peaceful New Age music' (its critics call it 'pastiche music', but never mind) which includes:

- Celtic harp music
- Sacred music (such as the Gregorian chant of Benedictine monks)
- Meditation music (such as Sheila Marchant Barish's 'Planetary Person' – 'original transcendent music of self-insight expanding into planetary awareness with the inner essence cosmic voice . . . a fully orchestrated experience you'll never forget')
- Space music (originated by Sun Ra)
- Natural sounds (e.g. whales mating under the Antarctic ice)
- New synthesizer music
- New mystic music (in fact anything with the prefix 'new' in front of it)

Inclusion of words like 'Planetary', 'Natural' and 'World' in the title indicates that you are on the right 'track'.

The more seriously musical go for the minimalist school such as Steve Reich, Terry Riley and Philip Glass, a Tibetan Buddhist whose best known work is a four-hour 'opera' entitled *Einstein on the Beach*. Genuine ethnic music from Africa, Asia and Latin America, such as gamelan chimes from Bali, chanting from the Bear Tribe, Tibetan and Andean wind instruments, is also popular.

Medieval and Renaissance dance music is good, and Albinoni is much the most popular of the classicals.

ATs quite frequently write their own folk music, using song titles like 'Instant Bliss' or 'The Guru in Your Life is You' (see below).

Instant Bliss

2. If you wanna fix your body
   Psychosynchronise your soul,
   Throw out that ageing preacher,
   Put your guru on the dole.

3. Zoom off in new directions,
   Sans sagacious interjections
   Day trips to meet your maker,
   In a handy plastic shaker,
   We're a cosmic Freddie Laker.

Chorus:

Meditation's procrastination.
Give up the Tao, the time is now.
Push the button, then, and then . . .
Instant bliss. Instant bliss.

4. Packaged evolution
   Tells the Buddha where to go.
   Electrocution's revolution
   This one is the final show.

5. It's atomized religion
   Scientifically designed
   To organize your Karma
   And undermine your mind.

Chorus:

Meditation's procrastination.
Give up the Tao, the time is now.
What you've been searching for is this.
It's cosmic joy, it's instant bliss
In
In
In
stant
Bliss

The Guru in Your Life is You

R.Valentine

2. Participate in psychodrama
Filmed in glorious traumarama,
Tune in on cosmic energy,
Freak out on planetary schemes,
Scare your friends with primal screams,
On the Ashram floor you'll find reality.

3. But I can't seem to get the hang,
of the balancing of yin and yang,
Acufracture makes me so afraid,
The stars just throw me into gloom,
With apocalyptic doom,
And the only fortune's the one
my guru's made.

4. I'm so sick of my brown rice diet,
And I want to yell at peace and quiet,
I'm I-I Ching to throw I Ching away,
I'm giving up these cosmic trips,
To get right back to fish and chips,
And forty fags and six pints every day.

5. When they offer you enlightenment
What they're selling is up-tightenment,
'Cos nobody can tell what's truly true,
'Cos really there's just you and me,
Two doggies round the cosmic tree,
And in the end you'll find
your guru's you.

Movies

ATs aren't strong on movies. Access to cinemas from the countryside and the small towns where they tend to live is pretty limited these days. So they often want to see films on TV. They would switch on for these:

Vanishing Point
Interiors (and other Woody Allen movies with Diane Keaton)
Nine to Five
A Passage to India
Diva
Gandhi (or other films set in India, especially Satyajit Ray films)
You Can't Take it with You (or any Capra movie – Frank, not Fritjof!)
Celine and Julie Go Boating
A Private Function (especially amusing to vegetarians)
Meetings with Remarkable Men (Peter Brook's somewhat chic restaging of Gurdjieff's autobiographical novel)
Jules et Jim
Woodstock (nostalgia – ATs have particularly fond memories of the shots of Bob Dylan's naked baby son on stage)
Easy Rider
Siddhartha
Walkabout
Duel
The Big Chill
The Wicker Man (paganism on a small Scottish island)

Anti-nuke films like:

The China Syndrome
Dr Strangelove
Silkwood

And sci-fi like:

2001
ET
Dark Star
Solaris
Silent Running
Invasion of the Body Snatchers

Even in the theatre, small is beautiful

Theatre

AT theatre reflects their interests. Visits to Stratford to see Shakespeare are confined to those occasions when distant American relations visit and insist on treating you. More their line is the muesli belt alternative theatre which will be putting on a play like:

> *A Fistful of Lentils* – In the far distant future there has been a mass conversion to wholefoods. The meat and dairy industries find themselves in a state of crisis and use their power to win back declining markets. Fowl play is the name of the game.

Alternative cabarets are becoming very popular. Be prepared to be called to help out in the act, standing on the stage while performers throw burning brands to each other with you in between them, and being 'supportive' and 'understanding' when the juggler drops the balls. Don't relax too much, though . . . be on your alert to walk out if the new act doesn't know the drill and slips into sexist or racist jokes. Top score if you see your favourite cabaret group before they get on Channel 4.

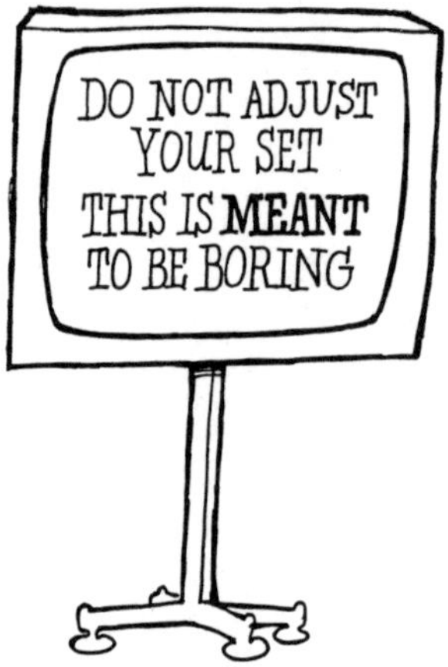

TV

It's best not to admit to watching TV. Better still, claim not to have one. If you *do* have one it's okay to have colour ('the nature programmes look so much better'). As a general rule, stick strictly to these programmes and the anthropological ones (of the 'How-Kalahari-bushmen-survive-two-weeks-on-three-ants-and-a-grasshopper' variety). Also popular:

The Good Life (ATs don't live in Surbiton so they can laugh at it)
The Jewel in the Crown (brings back memories of India)
Dr Who
Edge of Darkness (a thriller that made Gaia a household word)
and anything late on Channel 4: interviews with Buddhist monks, programmes on male sexuality, or Bolivian mask-making.

Some ATs are getting into computers, for which a TV or 'monitor' is okay. ATs don't slay aliens, but play 'cut the fence' at Greenham – 'Base Invaders'.

Sports and Leisure

Competitive sport is not something ATs go in for. Running marathons is completely out and so is jogging, though a school of thought allows it for meditation purposes – having one's own space. A few describe it as 'active rebirthing', or getting high (Arthur Ashe-style) on your own endomorphines.

Some of the more sociable sports are okay, though, particularly:

Tennis
Cricket
Swimming (but not competition racing). AT women never wear bikinis: swimming must be nude (both sexes) or in proper one-piece suits.
Skiing has a very 'jet-set' image still, but cross-country skiing is different (and okay).

vords into ploughshares: ATs use ex-military parachutes for cooperative games

Rock-climbing and hill-walking are both popular, hill-walking for its closeness to nature, rock-climbing for its closeness to death (and the meditative state this induces).

Hot-air-ballooning and hang-gliding (rich trendies) are out, but gliding is okay (very quiet and not so dangerous).

Long-distance cycling, and traversing rough ground on mountain bikes is popular for a little heart-in-mouth excitement.

Cooperative or 'new games', are becoming very popular. Played with enormous 'earth balls' or ex-military parachutes painted in bright colours, they can involve dozens (occasionally hundreds) of people, and given the space can take up an entire park.

Inner games, e.g. 'Inner tennis', are popular.

Also Zen football (there is no goal).

Sporting ATs also have *Golf in the Kingdom* on their bookshelf, an American treatise on 'Zen in the art of golf'.

Body, mind and spirit

Integrating body, mind and spirit is the ultimate aim of the AT and an enormous industry has developed to service this desire. Many ATs work in it. The term used by ATs for this development is the Human Potential Movement. It manifests in a bewildering variety of forms, many developed on the west coast of the USA – the Esalen Institute in California is the mecca of the Human Potential Movement, and Marin County, just across the Golden Gate Bridge from San Francisco, is where the greatest concentration of therapists, healers, mystics and gurus on earth is to be found. The mixture of Californian try-anything-once-wackiness combined with various oriental practices that have crossed the Pacific have combined to produce an extremely potent brew. Over here, the uninitiated soon get overwhelmed – a visitor to parts of the Body-Mind-Spirit Festival experiences the atmosphere of a medieval bazaar crowded with anxious seekers after various kinds of love and reassurance, and people selling them. The AT can see through all this stuff, but nevertheless likes to keep an open mind and try fresh things (especially if newly imported from Marin).

The Human Potential Movement has its fashionable therapies and therapists, its gurus and aspiring gurus, its frauds and its charlatans. The question is, how to pick a winner and stay ahead of the pack. For the spiritually inclined, various combinations of therapy and Eastern mysticism are now available. The best known of these are the 'orange people', followers of Bhagwan Shree Rajneesh – a fifty-four-year-old former philosophy professor turned guru, whose Ashram in Poona attracted thousands in the 1970s. Sometimes known as 'the rich man's guru', he moved in 1981 to a 64,000-acre ranch near Antelope, Oregon. Followers, known as Sanyasins, use a synthesis of body-mind techniques – encounter, bio-energetics, massage, Eastern meditation, yoga and sufi dancing. (They're very into looking good, vanity blended with spiritual search.) 'Dynamic' meditation involves (among other things) jumping up and down shouting 'hoo'. Lots of hugging. Free sexual expression is important, though the AIDS scare has caused havoc among Sanyasins in the US. Bhagwan has recently issued instructions discouraging kissing, and recommending the

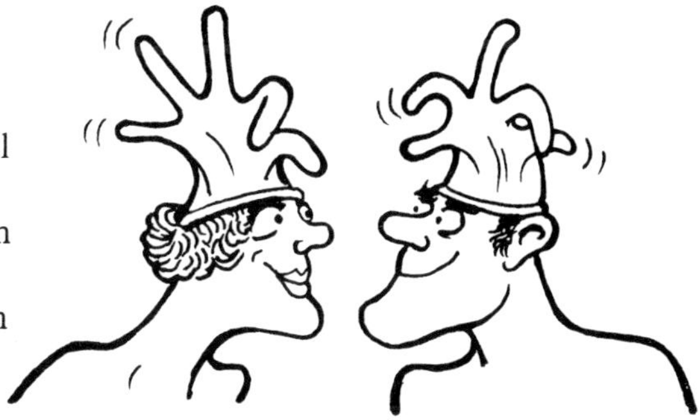

wearing of rubber gloves during sexual intercourse. The group has experienced considerable hostility from the US authorities, and Rajneesh was arrested while trying to leave the US in 1985 after a much publicized split in the sect.

Yoga is a practice involving body, mind and spirit. Any self-respecting AT will have done some kind of yoga, and probably still practise it. Aikido, Tai Chi and, for the more advanced, Kendo are also popular.

All these have historical links with Buddhism. Buddhism is *the* religious practice of the AT. It's more a psychology than a religion, emphasizing reason, compassion, self-knowledge, and self-responsibility. Based on the realizations of Gautama Buddha who, in the fifth century BC in India, declared the Four Noble Truths (short version):

1. Life involves considerable dissatisfaction and suffering.
2. The cause of suffering is desire, greed and self-centredness.
3. Freedom from desire is liberation.
4. The way to overcome all this and achieve liberation is through an eight-fold path: right understanding, right purpose, right speech, right action, right livelihood, right effort, right attention and right concentration.

The path is known as the Middle Way (Tolkienistic Buddhists sometimes call their houses things like 'Middle Way'). Much AT thinking is influenced by Buddhism, hence the whole 'right livelihood' biz. There are various types of Buddhism. Popular among ATs is Zen (at least they *claim* it to be Zen). Anti-intellectual, stressing direct experience, it actually requires great discipline – many hours of formless meditation struggling with 'koans' – riddles with no answer given by your teacher, e.g. 'What is the sound of one hand clapping?' Inevitably, I suppose, a book of 'answers' to the koans has been published in California, for those who haven't got the time to hang around for decades waiting for enlightenment. The 'answer' to that one is 'silence' in case you are curious – easy when you don't think

......and don't overdo the brown rice

about it. Needless to say, any true Zen teacher will tell you that there are no answers – everything just *is*. Best known Zen Buddhist in Britain: Pooh Bear. Up and coming on the fast track is Nichirin Buddhism. It's big in the US and it's catching on here. It's strong on chanting, and is ideal for the AT who wants to make it. Not afraid of success, achievement or style, it's pushy, even proselytising. Being a Nichirin Buddhist, you can be ritzy, glitzy, famous *and* fulfilled; no need for begging bowls and shaved heads here. It's for the ATs who dress Katharine Hamnett style (she's interested too) or who might have read *Tomorrow* had it survived. It's the new brand of the 1980s – Designer Buddhism.

Hinduism also comes from the East, and involves yoga. Hinduism isn't popular amongst ATs these days (though it was in the 1960s – remember the Beatles going off to India to see the Maharishi). Some of its Western off-shoots have got a bad name: TM (Transcendental Meditation) – what the Beatles did – has largely fallen out of fashion except with the US air force (perhaps that's why). So too has the Divine Light Mission – Guru Maharaji's group. He was popular in the 1970s with a certain crowd, but his following is much more low key these days. His propensity for driving around in Cadillacs alienated some (though for some reason Bhagwan's love affairs with Rolls-Royces – he had ninety-three at the last count – doesn't seem to have had the same effect on *his* followers). The Krishna Consciousness Society are the 'Hare Krishna' chanting crowd to be seen regularly in Oxford Street.

They might be described as Hindu fundamentalists: when asked why they appear as they do – ochre robed, shaven headed, pig-tailed and banging tambourines – they reply, 'Because that is what God looks like.' However they are most un-Hindu, in that they seek for converts (and have had considerable success among younger Americans looking for a certain kind of absolutism). They are friendly folk (you can get free food from them at festivals) but have never been an AT cult (all that chanting in the West End is a bit too public and shaven heads aren't very sexy). The Hindu words 'guru' and 'karma' have passed into the language, both used in a much debased form (as in 'Bill Shankley, guru of football club managers').

Sufism – essentially the mystical side of Islam – is becoming increasingly popular, mostly through the writings of Idries Shah, a charismatic descendant of the prophet Mohammed. It makes great use of the Sufi technique of the teaching story, particularly those concerning the mystic simpleton Nasrudin. Idries Shah spotted the drift towards 'spiritual tourism' among the young inner-directed in the West some years ago, and Nasrudin has something to say on the subject:

> Nasrudin was taking a donkey-load of grapes to market. Groups of small children kept begging grapes, but he only gave them a very small handful each. 'You are mean, Nasrudin,' they shouted. 'Not at all,' said the Mulla. 'I am doing this to illustrate the silliness of children. All these grapes taste the same. Once you have had some you know what all the rest are like. So it doesn't matter if you have many or just a few.'

Bahai – relatively recent (nineteenth century) – originated in what is now Iran. Adherents are very open and friendly and believe in the fundamental unity of all world religions. One American group in the mid-1970s decided they did not like the way things were going in the USA, got out a map of the world and looked for the most undisturbed, god-forsaken spot on earth to emigrate to for a lifetime's peace and quiet. They chose – yes, you guessed it – the Falkland Islands.

Gurdjieff called his method 'The Fourth Way'. Gurdjieff was a 'vogue guru', highly unconventional, but his followers have retreated into conformity and isolation. However his writings, and those of his one-time colleague P. D. Ouspensky, are still very popular among seekers after truth.

For those in the Christian tradition, the Quakers are undoubtedly the most popular. Their candle-lit vigils are events to be 'seen at'. Roman Catholicism has something of a following, too, being strong on mystical chanting (e.g. Gregorian chant), and 'liberation theology' is causing a revival of interest in the more politically conscious ATs.

The AT's close connection with nature and commitment to the earth has led to considerable interest in the mother goddess, earth mysteries etc. That is one reason why Glastonbury is such a popular spot to live (many believe it to be surrounded by a ten-mile-across terrestrial zodiac immemorially inscribed upon the landscape), and celebrating pagan festivals is so common. The 'earth goddess' worship, variously described as 'paganism', 'pantheism', 'radical eco-paganism' or even 'eco-naturalist taoism', has generated a number of publications including *Pipes of P.A.N.* (Pagans against Nukes) and *Wood and Water* (both feminist-orientated), *The Ley Hunter*, *Ancient Mysteries*, and the *New Celtic Review*. No formal sects, though; ritual is do-it-yourself.

Certain groups, which combine authoritarianism with money-making and are largely American in origin, have latched on to the mystical element in the 'New Age' and turned it to their own advantage. This materialistic outlook on the world has been adopted by several cults/sects/therapies with southern Californian origins (must be something to do with the climate). Foremost among these are:

REBIRTHING. See box.

SCIENTOLOGY. Controversial organization founded by L. Ron Hubbard. UK base near East Grinstead. It got massive press coverage in the 1960s and early 1970s when the government banned foreigners entering the country to study scientology. It has taken a much lower profile since then. Hubbard's writings give an impression not of spirituality but of a sci-fi author creating his visions on an ever more majestic scale.

EST (ERHARD SEMINAR TRAINING). A well-known outfit which uses intensive aggressive encounter techniques to drive out rational processes and shock people into seeing and accepting what they really are. It often has the effect of making people highly individualistic, competitive and desirous of 'success' in the status quo sense. Vastly expensive: £200+ for two weekends. Like Bhagwan and Guru Maharaji, Werner Erhard is heavily into cars. He goes for lots of racing cars, and likes trying them out.

EXEGESIS, similar to EST, describes itself as being 'in the *business* of transformation' and a very successful business too. It has been described as 'making EST look like a vicarage tea-party' and

awe-struck observers have commented that after Exegesis, 'spaced out hippies end up wearing suits and ties and working for IBM.'

All of these have an ideological link (Werner Erhard admits to drawing heavily on Scientology materials for his EST trainings) – what ATs call a 'left-brain' approach, hard, masculine, hierarchical – and are wary.

So how do you find the 'in therapies'? Well, anything to do with AT role models – William Reich, R. D. Laing, Arthur Janov or Fritz Perls – are good, even chic. These include:

- Bio-energetics
- Reichian and neo-Reichian body work
- Rolfing
- Encounter
- Gestalt
- Psychodrama
- Bio-dynamic psychology
- Postural integration
- Various regression therapies, including: primal therapy, primal integration and intensive rhythm therapy

There are many others, but current fashion leaders are:

- Voice dialogue (developed out of Gestalt and known as VD to its adherents)
- Neuro linguistic programming (claims to have videoed all the other therapies, studied all the effective bits, and synthesized them into one super therapy – NLP. Practitioners precisely copy your body movements in order to get 'in tune' with you)

Much more in the AT's line are forms of natural healing with long histories. ATs collect them like other people collect antiques, the older and more well rubbed the better.

- Acupuncture (and acupressure)
- Alexander technique
- Homeopathy (patronized by the Royal Family)
- Herbalism
- Naturapathy
- Aromatherapy
- Reflexology (foot massage)
- Applied kinesiology (touch for health)
- Chiropractic (like osteopathy but much gentler)

Rebirthing

Rebirthing was developed by southern Californian property developer Leonard Orr. He prefers to call it 'the scientific pentecostal experience' and claims it to be the 'physical experience of the infinite being'. Rebirthing combines simple yoga techniques and breathing exercises in order to experience the emotional and physical sensations of birth, childhood, or past lives. Like all the best discoveries, Orr's Great Leap Forward was made from his bathtub. He found that by submerging his friends in the bath (or 'hot tub') for three to four hours (deep breathing through a snorkel) he could produce in them a semi-paralytic state of regression to infancy. Startled that the effect of being with him for four hours could be so devastating and at the same time apparently enjoyable to his clients, Orr seized his opportunity, concluding that 'my presence has commercial value'. He swiftly moved his enterprise on to dry land, breathing hard. 'I stopped sleeping with women who hadn't been rebirthed,' he claimed, 'after I woke up a couple of times to find them paralysed in bed beside me.'

Rebirthers have an enterprise philosophy. Each of us, they say, has endless potential to choose every circumstance of our life. Thus an Ethiopian peasant has chosen to starve, an Argentinian has decided to disappear. If 'positively affirmed', universal and abundant wealth will be ours (and Orr encourages a belief in physical immortality which gets round the problem of what to do with it all when you die). Prosperity features highly. If you believe you deserve to be rich, then 'prosper' others. Money will flow through your pockets. Especially, prosper your rebirther (anywhere between £7 and £50 per hour – you choose). If you don't prosper them properly you're accused of 'poverty consciousness'.

Some participants have learned to protect themselves from this sales pitch by concentrating on other things. One has described his method as 'acting out my Castaneda-at-the-feet-of-Don-Juan fantasy'. He went on to haggle over the price of the treatment and, ultimately realizing the power of affirmation, stumped his rebirther with the irrefutably true proposition, 'Everything is free', backed up for good measure with 'I always get what I want'. It will cause chaos if it catches on.

Orr is no longer the only guru produced by the rebirthers. A genuine Indian mystic has now joined the carnival. Babaji lives in an ashram in north India, and rebirthers travel out to sit at his feet. Apparently he is known for saying nothing but simply *hitting* supplicants (who love it). Rebirthers in England can sometimes be seen selling 75p calendars for £7.50 to buy him woolly jumpers (it's cold in the hills), or knitting him woolly socks to send as presents. Strange necessities for someone who claims both to be a remanifestation of Jesus *and* to be able to rematerialize anywhere in the world.

- Bach flower remedies (a delightful system involving steeping flowers in water, extracting their essence and mixing the results into little bottles. Best known is 'Rescue Remedy' for shocks and upsets of all kinds)
- Medicine wheel (native American). Shamans have replaced gurus as the true source of wisdom in the 1980s.
- Massage in its various forms is almost too common to be AT any more, though none the worse for that; the popular conception of massage, fostered by those 1930s movies, that it is only suitable for gangsters who go into steam baths to be vigorously pummelled by massive Turks has changed a lot. Massage workshops are very in.

In America holistic health isn't confined to humans. Psychology for dogs is available in Los Angeles, and members of the recently formed American Veterinary Holistic Medical Association will treat the 'whole dog' for you with all the therapies available to humans over here. It's only a matter of time . . .

ATs like to know what's going to happen next, which has led to interest in various forms of divination, and other ways of predicting the future. Astrology is the best known expression of this, and there's a lot more to it than what you read in newspapers. Many ATs take it seriously, even having their own astrologer, as well as their own therapist. ATs put their transits in their diaries (and when things go wrong blame Saturn). AT men who really get into astrology have a tendency to project their fantasies of their ideal partner on to that person's birth chart. AT women plot their moon phases to synchronize their natural cycles.

Astrologer-types and therapy-types often mingle in the AT world, but how do you tell them apart? By their body language, naturally.

After gatherings you'll see that astrologers wave goodbye to each other and wash up their own mugs. Transpersonal psychologists, on the other hand, hug each other when they part (and exhibit separation anxieties) and wash up each other's mugs – watch out next time . . .

A recent development from astrology is Astro-cartography. Basically this involves using a computer to draw up your 'personal power points' on a world map, the 'places where lifelong opportunities exist for you to find love, prosperity, creativity and any other human potential'. You can change your life by changing your address, is the claim. Well, anyway, Jimmy Carter's map had his Mars (symbolizing aggression) and Jupiter (religious preoccupation) passing over Teheran . . . he should have known better.

What are you really worth?

Most therapies are about increasing people's self-esteem and self-valuation – but what is a person's 'self-worth'? It depends on how you look at it. It's generally believed that the raw material needed to make up a 150 lb person would only amount to about £5-worth of carbon, nitrogen, hydrogen, oxygen, sulphur, phosphorus and other elements. On the other hand, other estimates come out with some very different figures, like:

£500	in cholesterol
£650	in fibrinogen
£2,000	in haemoglobin
£4,000	in albumin
£25,000	in prothrombin and the immunoglobin 1G
£100,000	of myoglobin

and that's just a small part . . .

Other well known forms of divination include Tarot and I Ching but more obscure forms are practised, too. These include:

Aeromancy	divination by cloud shapes
Alectryomancy	bird pecks grains of corn from letter of alphabet
Apantomancy	chance meeting of animals
Capnomancy	patterns of smoke rising from a fire
Causiomomancy	study of objects placed in a fire
Cromniomancy	finding significance in onion sprouts
Hippomancy	based on stamping of horses
Onychomancy	patterns of fingernails in sunlight
Phyllarhodomancy	sounds made by slapping rose petals against the hand (developed by the ancient Greeks)
Tiromancy	systems of divination involving cheese.

Self-improvement isn't confined to kicking and screaming on the floor all the time. ATs take the intellectual side very seriously too. Although it certainly isn't necessary to have gone to university to be an AT, quite a few have. Quite a few more have gone to art school, or done craft-based courses – Dartington College of Art is *the* place if you did. A lot of ATs failed the 11+ (the first beginnings of questioning society), being slow developers, but ended up going to college. Almost anything goes as regards university (except Exeter and St Andrews – Sloanes only). Something like nuclear physics at Imperial College (gives you a head start on the 'New Physics' scene) or religious studies at Sussex (opportunity to study Buddhism *and* get paid for it) are particularly good. 'Man and his image of nature' (*pace* the sexist title) is a particularly AT course for Sussex graduates to have done. Your thesis title was something like 'Does Don Juan really fly?'

But self-improvement doesn't end with graduation. While others may do practical car mechanics, flower arranging or German evening classes, ATs go in for courses with titles like:

'Practical Egyptian magic'
'Experiencing your plants on the astral plane'
'Professional journal writing' (ATs have a fantasy that their journal – *not* diary – will be the publishing event of the year when they are eighty-five)
'Firewalking for beginners' ('the course will include skydiving, rappelling and many other processes to help people overcome their limitations')
'Coming to terms with the shadow'
'Esoteric aspects of breastfeeding'
'A homeowner's guide to other lifetimes' (I'm not sure what's available to council tenants)
'Who on earth am I?' (growth astrology)
'We are stardust, we are golden' (trance, hypnosis and biodynamic therapy)

For those who cannot keep up with the pace, it *is* possible to escape. Those with the money and the time should hot-foot it over to California for an:

Egyptian Experiential Weekend

Arrive at the beautiful Oasis – a serene setting in the Russian River Wine Country adorned with exotic birds and animals. Meet your hosts, Lora Vigne and Paul Ramses, over a beautiful buffet and get to know each other around an outdoor fireplace or in a hot spa or cool pool. Morning: after breakfast, be guided gently back to an Egyptian lifetime real or imagined, and gain insight into who you really are. A short walk through an orchard for a picnic on the river. Afternoon: a period of rest and relaxation, on the grounds or under the meditation tree. Evening: an ancient Egyptian feast followed by entertainment by award-winning Troupe Mandala from Mt Shasta and the Gypsy Caravan, a local troupe of dancers you won't soon forget. Enjoy a peaceful sleep. After breakfast a tarot card reading for all participants. Lunch, then final affirmations and fond farewells.

It's only $100 for the two days (plus the air fare).

Closer to home, but further away too, disappear into a 'relaxation tank' for a while. The tank is filled with a salt water solution so concentrated that muscle control is impossible, and your body can float in darkness and womb-like oblivion. The experience lasts an hour and you emerge limbs quivering. Videos are optional during this birth/death simulation. They consist chiefly of prancing deer . . . nature is in.

The social calendar

Other people's lives revolve around annual events like Ascot, Henley, Cowes or the start of the grouse season. ATs need their social events to be 'seen' at too. For the past few years *the* event has been the 'Festival of Mind, Body and Spirit' in London in early July. Sadly, this 'ideal soul exhibition' is now defunct, to be replaced by the relatively untried 'Festival of the Spirit', and the regional versions like the 'Earth Spirit Festival' in Malvern. It remains to be seen whether these can ever be an adequate replacement. 'New Age' events have yet to acquire that patina of age needed to make them into institutions, though some are trying, notably:

The Dartington Spring Conference
Findhorn Conferences and Arts Festival (going to these shows you're rich)

The Schumacher lectures
Mystics and Scientists gathering (implies that you are one or the other – or both)
TOES (The Other Economic Summit, you can pretend you're at the leading edge of the 'New Economics')

For those summery open-air festivals try:

Cosmic Bears Picnic on the Ridgeway near Silbury Hill (early July)
Elephant Fayre (Cornwall, July, and now a major alternative arts festival. Set in the grounds of a pedigree stately home, it was a port in the Bronze Age, the traffic-free city of canvas with its theatres, shops and restaurants, street entertainers and strolling minstrels, evokes the spirit of Woodstock).

Social events to be 'seen' at (not Henley, Ascot or Cowes)

Rougham Tree Fair (held in Suffolk in the early autumn)
Hood Fayre (Totnes, Devon, September)

and for those who still like their rock music hard, and the crowds big,

CND's June festival at Glastonbury. The Green Gathering at Pilton, Somerset, in August is another institution that has fallen foul of the law, economics and over popularity, but it may return.

For the more mystically inclined:

The Glastonbury Earth Mysteries gathering, twice yearly at Beltane (Spring) and Lugnasadh (Autumn), described as celebrations of nature sun, sky and Avalon. They're open to gardeners, leyhunters, pagans, healers, or dowsers; child, elder, tree person, shaman, therapier or any cosmic 'being'.

Christmas is replaced by the winter solstice and the mid-summer solstice is celebrated at Stonehenge, though the Avebury/Silbury complex is enjoying a revival as Stonehenge gets so overcrowded (mainly by police).

Autumn sees festivals associated with the magic mushroom. Biggest and longest established of these is the psilocybin festival in mid-Wales (precise location changes each year). Affectionately known as the psilly fair.

Local events are also popular, including:

The Peaceful Ley-hunter's Picnic (September)

AT events attract leprechauns, goblins, imps, trolls . . . and Alice's cat

Magical mystery tour at Chanctonbury Ring, Sussex (ditto)
The Cadders Hill Fairie Fair, Norfolk. This one is open to 'Leprechauns, goblins, imps, trolls, will-o-the-wisps, brownies, pixies, mermaids, elves and giants'. Humans can come along too, entrance free if in costume. Much barter, and mushrooms, no electrics; descendant of the Albion Fayre.

Keeping up to the mark

In the constant striving for the integration of body, mind and spirit, the holistic approach, the Gaian perspective, and the non-competitive relationship to your fellow human being, pitfalls can open up for the unwary. To keep up to the mark make sure you don't let slip un-right-on ideas, or be seen with or doing un-right-on things. In certain circles this is known as the 'street credibility test'. You are slipping if you:

- Trade in your investment in socially responsible unit trusts or pension funds for unsocially responsible ones, when their performance slips

- Proposition a female executive over drinks at a Business Network Seminar (you are taking the invitation to 'make connections' too literally)
- Replace your 'deux chevaux' with a Ford Fiesta
- Are caught with copies of

  The Habitat catalogue

  Newsweek

  Options (you may be able to read about AT role model Stewart Brand – *Whole Earth Catalog* compiler, *Co-evolution Quarterly* editor – in the gossip column these days, but it's selling out)
- Don't renew your subscription to Friends of the Earth
- Join the National Trust
- Join the SDP
- Start buying Crabtree and Evelyn conserves instead of making your own
- Start referring to Krishnamurti as a guru
- Introduce your partner as 'my wife', or worse still, 'the wife' (if male) or 'my better half' (if female)
- Buy a Cuisenart blender/mixer
- Admit to not liking the taste of 'grain coffee'
- Find more than a third of your wardrobe is bought from Laura Ashley
- Are overheard saying that you think Mrs Thatcher's small business promotion policies are 'on the right lines'
- Buy a video
- Go on holiday on the Canary Islands
- Join BUPA
- Go to the Habitat sale
- Start buying household equipment made of plastic
- Use a word processor to write your book
- Buy a cordless telephone, or join Cellnet
- Are spotted with the *AA Book of the Car*, *New English Bible*, *The Ascent of Man* or anything by Reader's Digest on your bookshelf, or any cookbooks by Robert Carrier in the kitchen
- Buy shares in any Thatcher sell-off (e.g. British Telecom, British Gas or TSB)

AT view of history

BIBLICAL TIMES	Noah invents monogamy. Whale saves Jonah, reciprocal basis for Greenpeace established.
GREEK CIVILIZATION	Greeks invent windmills.
ROMAN EMPIRE	Romans invent 'hot tubs'. Lazarus invents 'rebirthing'. Jesus invents Transactional Analysis, rescuer-persecutor-victim triangle. St Sebastian discovers acupuncture.
DARK AGES	Early Christians discover New Age holy sites at Glastonbury and Iona. Canute discovers wave power. King Alfred discovers woodburning stoves.
MEDIEVAL TIMES	York mystery cycle first performed – psychodrama invented. 'Princes in the Tower' bring meditation to Britain.
ENGLISH REVOLUTION	Diggers invent allotments. Charles I discovers disadvantages of the separation of mind and body.
FRENCH REVOLUTION	Therapeutic value of knitting first recognized.
ROMANTIC PERIOD	Blake makes talking to plants acceptable.
AMERICAN FRONTIER PERIOD	Lewis and Clark invent backpacking in the wilderness. 49ers invent 'prosperity consciousness' in California's Bay area.
VICTORIAN PERIOD	Oliver Twist invents claiming.

AT quiz: are you alternative?

1. Your local vicarage is bought by a previously unknown (to you) Buddhist sect. Do you:

   a) Organize the village petition calling for the planning committee to refuse a change of use
   b) Try to spread rumours amongst community members that the place is haunted
   c) Invite the abbot to tea
   d) Join it

2. An unexpected legacy from a maiden aunt includes a controlling share in the family vinegar and pickles manufacturing company. Do you:

   a) Sell your controlling interest to a rival multi-national food-processing company and retire to the Bahamas on the proceeds
   b) Hand over your shareholding to a trust controlled by the workers
   c) Move into the managing director's chair yourself and launch a new product range in wholefood mustards, organic chutneys and sugar-free jams
   d) Bully the other members of the family into floating the company on the stock exchange and use the capital to diversify into acid rain and other pollution control equipment manufacture

3. A young man accosts you in the street on one of your rare visits to London, and offers you a 'pound of Jamaican'. Do you:

   a) Buy it thinking it is coffee
   b) Buy it thinking it is marijuana
   c) Haggle over the price
   d) Ask him if he knows a source of organic carob beans

4. You are invited to an old schoolfriend's wedding. Do you:
   a) Accept the invitation and turn up in a morning suit
   b) Accept the invitation and turn up in bare feet and a lunghi
   c) Decline the invitation but crash the reception anyway
   d) Decline the invitation on a postcard saying 'nuclear family no thanks'

5. Your elder brother is arrested on a drugs charge. Do you:
   a) Find the best lawyer you can afford to defend him
   b) Visit him in the cells and ask where the stash is
   c) Phone your grandmother and suggest she changes her will in your favour
   d) Offer to appear for the prosecution

6. You inherit a productive 100-acre farm in the West Country. Do you:
   a) Submit a planning application to build 250 houses on it
   b) Install a manager with instructions to maximize its profitability by intensive agriculture
   c) Move down to it yourself and run it on organic principles
   d) Turn it into a health farm specializing in natural diet regimes

7. Your case comes up in court for your arrest at a peace camp. Do you:
   a) Take a day's sick leave
   b) Take a day's holiday
   c) Start a fighting fund at work to pay your fine
   d) Ask your boss if you can use his office for a press conference in the lunch hour

8. A man from MI5 approaches you after a university friend who has applied for a job at the BBC is positively vetted. Do you:
   a) Show him photos of you both on an anti-Vietnam war demonstration
   b) Pretend you never knew your friend
   c) Impress the plod by taking him out to lunch
   d) Seize the opportunity and offer to spy on fellow members of your peace group

9. You return home earlier than expected from a holiday and find your partner in bed with someone else. Do you:

a) Apologize profusely and close the door
b) Threaten to slay them both with the ritual Japanese sword hanging on the wall
c) Ruin their fun by dissolving into tears
d) Make a pot of herb tea and sit round the kitchen table sharing everyone's feelings

10. An ex-communard shows up on your doorstep, homeless and accompanied by partner and three children. Do you:

a) Give them the address of the night shelter
b) Stuff them all into one room and drive them down to Social Security the following morning
c) Evict your unemployed son and his girlfriend to make room for them
d) Get wildly drunk listening to old Bob Dylan records and give them the keys to your Welsh cottage in the morning

11. Your sister phones to say she's going 'orange'. Do you:

a) Commiserate and comment that you had noticed there was a nasty strain of hepatitis around at the moment
b) Offer to knit her a red and maroon scarf
c) Hire a private investigator to 'rescue' her
d) Sell your story to the *News of the World*

12. It is time to replace your ageing 'deux chevaux'. Do you:

a) Buy another
b) Trade it in for a Volvo Estate
c) Start a vehicle-sharing co-op
d) Try and keep it going for just one more year

13. (*for women only*) The air conditioning in your favourite wholefood cafe breaks down on a hot summer day. Customers start stripping off. Do you:

a) Order an iced tea

b) Offer to repair the equipment
c) Complain to the management about men taking their T-shirts off
d) Take your own T-shirt off

14. (*for men only*) A theatre performance turns out to be for women only. Do you:
a) Accept your non-admission gracefully
b) Threaten to sue under the Sex Discrimination Act
c) Offer to help run the crèche
d) Go home and come back dressed in drag

ANSWERS

1.	a) 0	b) 0	c) 5	d) 2	8.	a)0	b)0	c)0	d)0
2.	a) 0	b) 3	c) 5	d) 1	9.	a)0	b)3	c)0	d)2
3.	a) 2	b) 1	c) 3	d) 0	10.	a)0	b)0	c)0	d)2
4.	a) 0	b) 1	c) 3	d) 0	11.	a)1	b)5	c)0	d)0
5.	a) 3	b) 1	c) 0	d) 0	12.	a)1	b)0	c)3	d)5
6.	a) 0	b) 0	c) 2	d) 5	13.	a)2	b)5	c)0	d)5
7.	a) 0	b) 1	c) 3	d) 5	14.	a)1	b)0	c)5	d)3

SCORING

Over 30: Very good, but you must try and control that competitive streak

16–30: You are too trendy for words

1–15: You are an unreconstructed capitalist, and probably in the Tory Cabinet

0: You realized that there are no right answers and refused to do the quiz – congratulations – you are truly alternative

The AT alphabet

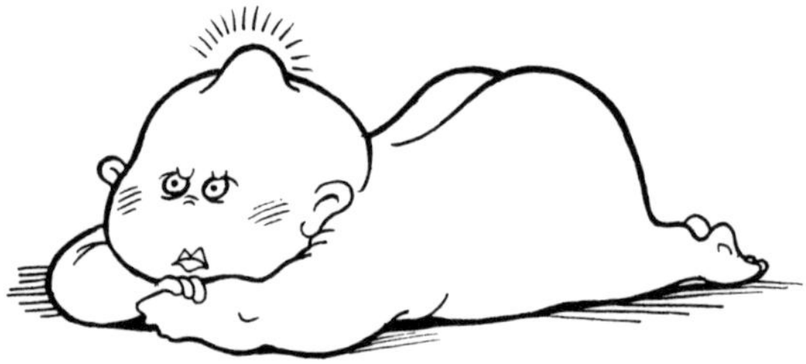

A

Active Birth 'Mother-orientated' birth method. Developed in France by Michel Odent. Involves walking around during labour, not lying down but giving birth in a squatting position. Very popular with ATs.
Acupuncture Chinese method of undermining multinational drug corporations.
Allotments Vital part of the whole AT identity. Patches of ground for growing your own vegetables. Allotment world can become quite exclusive and competitive as ATs vie with each other for the best crop of garlic (while their neighbours go for prize leeks).
Aquarian Conspiracy Name of best-selling book by American author Marilyn Ferguson. Promulgates the idea that the New Age (or 'Aquarian Age') is an unconscious conspiracy to change the world, that one day we'll all wake up ATs – it will have happened without our really noticing.
Astrology The timetable for personal and global transformation.

B

Beards All men have them, but some interfere with nature and cut them off. High proportion of beards among AT men. Rapidly going out of fashion among the feminist-influenced, androgynous under-thirty-fives. In Tasmania the AT beard stereotype was so strong that in 1983 when local environmentalists tried to stop a dam being built in a wilderness, locals beat up *any* men with beards who showed up in local pubs.

Black holes One of the glamorous concepts culled from the fringes of scientific research by ATs interested in consciousness expansion. Alternatively, last-ditch hope of individuals who wish not only to get off the planet but out of the entire universe.
Blissed out State of happy incoherence brought on by too much meditation.

C

Community ATs aspire to live in one, whether 'intentional' (i.e. communal house) or local, as in people who live in the area you move to.
Conservation Save piles of newspapers for people not to collect. Ditto jam jars, yoghurt pots, egg boxes.
Co-ops Alternative to hierarchies. ATs approve of co-ops, but more often dream about than do. Like 'community', co-ops is a right-on buzz word.
Counterculture Label given to the AT idea when it first started in California in the 1960s.

D

Dao Correct way to spell Tao. Synonym for 'Zen and the art of . . . '

E

$E=MC^2$ A twentieth-century mantra.
Energy ATs run their hi-fis on wind energy and their bodies on chi energy. (Same thing really, see $E=MC^2$.)
Esalen Institute Retirement home for ageing American professors who were casualties of the psychedelic sixties. Now the New Age enlightenment centre. In the old days people went east for enlightenment, now you go west.
Extraterrestrials See networking.

F

Findhorn Famous New Age spiritual centre, located in caravan park (but the idea of the 'planetary village' does not mean that the world will be covered in caravans).
Futon Vital piece of AT furniture, for sleeping on. Originates in Japan.

G

Gaia Seeing the planet as one interdependent living organism. The Gaian perspective is now the only acceptable AT view of the world.
Gestalt Popular AT therapy, taught at weekend seminars by intense Americans.
Global As in village. Invented by Marshall McLuhan.
Green As in 'the Greens' (political party in Germany). Anything with the adjective Green attached is okay.

H

Hi-tech ATs don't like it unless applied to renewable energy sources.
Hi touch Concept popularized in American cult book *Megatrends*, which argues that we are moving towards a hi-touch society. Evidence adduced includes everything from heart transplants to EST.
Holistic Seeing the connections in everything. Similar to Gaia.
Hot tubs Very large barrels chopped in half, full of warm water and people. Much in demand by rebirthers. Usually outdoors. Esalen Institute has several overlooking the Pacific Ocean.

I

I-Ching Sophisticated way of tossing coins to make a decision.

Intermediate technology Bicycles and windmills.
Interpersonal Sociological definition of murder, 'aggravated interpersonal altercation'.

J

Jacuzzi Indoor hot tub with bubbles.
Jesus Popular hero of the Piscean age.

K

Karma Principle that everything that you do comes back to you. Fate as a New Age boomerang.

L

Leading edge Concept popularized by *Aquarian Conspiracy* author, Marilyn Ferguson, and title of her magazine promoting the New Age in the USA.

Lunar Holistic calendar. Biodynamic gardeners plant their seeds according to the phases of the moon, astro-contraception ditto.

M

Mandala Diagrammatic systematization of the universe. Usually symmetrical, unlike the universe.
Marin Californian county just across the Golden Gate Bridge from San Francisco. World centre of the New Age, and per capita income of residents second highest in US.
Meditation An excuse for not greeting visitors. 'Marsha can't come down right now, she's meditating.'

Mega Big word for big, as in 'megatrends'.

N

Natural The opposite of plastic.
Networking Long word for talking to people.
Nostradamus Medieval seer, whose cryptic prophecies have an uncanny tendency to predict world events.

O

Orange Colour of the sunset, as worn by sanyasins (followers of Bhagwan).
Organic Carrots cultivated on compost, not chemicals.

P

Person As in whole, chair, spokes; formerly man.
Physics (new) The search for the theory of everything.
Planetary See Global; 'planetary village' invented at Findhorn.
Prosperity consciousness Convincing yourself you're good enough to charge over the odds for everything.

Q

Qaballah Early Jewish form of meta-programming.
Quaker Christian Buddhist.

R

Right livelihood Conducting business as if people mattered.
Right on What you've got to be to get . . .

S

Street credibility AT status. The leading edge of your local muesli belt.

Self Someone to love.
Social investing Otherwise known as 'socially responsible investing'. Putting all that inherited cash into right livelihood business. Making sure all your pounds are green.
Space Three kinds exist – outer, inner and personal.
Synergy 2 + 2 = 5.

T

TA Transactional analysis – early role-model identification system.
Tai Chi The Zen shuffle.
Tao Chinese for 'the way'. Replaces 'Zen and the art of . . . ' as the way of book-selling.
Tarot Cards for fortune-telling; as in 'The only fortune is the one my guru's made.'
Tibetan applause Way of showing appreciation without breaking the energy by clapping – put your hands in the air and shake them. Invented at Findhorn.
TOES The Other Economic Summit. Gathering of AT economic gurus, annual, in London. (See: places to be seen at.)

U

Unconscious Something you mess around with in therapy.

V

Vegetarianism The food you can cook for your dinner party to be on the safe side.
Vegan What your guests then announce they are.

Venusians See extraterrestrials.

W

Wales AT *lebensraum*.
Whales AT mascots. Some ATs save newspapers and milk bottle tops. All ATs save whales.
Windmills Large natural battery chargers.

X

X Symbol that ATs put beside Green Party candidates on ballot slips.

Y

Youth Something you try to preserve with . . .
Yoga Bending and stretching for health and vitality.
Yoghourt ATs' alternative to cream. Homemade variety festers in the best ATs' airing cupboards.

Z

Zen Incapable of definition.